50 Strategies for Experiential Learning:
Book One

50 Strategies
for Experiential Learning:
Book One

(Formerly *Affective Education: Strategies for Experiential Learning*)

Edited by

Louis Thayer
Eastern Michigan University

UNIVERSITY ASSOCIATES, INC.
8517 Production Avenue
P.O. Box 26240
San Diego, California 92126

Copyright © 1976 by International Authors, B.V.
Formerly titled *Affective Education: Strategies for Experiential Learning*
ISBN: 0-88390-108-0
Library of Congress Catalog Card Number 75-27735
Printed in the United States of America

Preface

After Kent Beeler and I became involved in the American Educational Research Association's Special Interest Group: Affective Aspects of Education, we decided to initiate a series of handbooks on affective education. Our goals for the annual conference programs were to encourage professionals to share ideas and strategies that had worked for them in establishing more humanistic learning environments. This publication is an outgrowth of the first handbook we edited on affective education, the *Handbook of Affective Tools and Techniques for the Educator*.

The close collaboration that Kent and I shared in editing the handbooks for the Special Interest Group was not possible on this book. I completed the major portion of the project during my year as a Visiting Fellow at the Center for Studies of the Person in La Jolla, California. Although Kent did not assist in editing *50 Strategies for Experiential Learning*, he is one of its major contributors.

The people involved in the Special Interest Group and those represented in this book are involved in and committed to affective education—they are concerned about the person in the learning process. It is exciting to learn of the numerous individuals who are committed to making educational settings more humanistic for learners.

There are many people who have contributed to making this book possible. I extend my gratitude and appreciation to the following people for their part in the process: the contributors, for sharing their ideas and for believing that affective education should be an integral part of the educational learning process; Micheline and Yves de Passillé-Sylvestre of St. Adele, Quebec, well-known artists in Canada and the United States, for the use of the "Symbolic Man" on the cover; Bill Beckley, art director at Graphic Communications, Plymouth, Michigan, for the original cover design; Sandy Schwartzenberger and Arlene Phillips, secretaries in the College of Education at Eastern Michigan University, for their secretarial assistance; J. William Pfeiffer and John E. Jones, president and vice-president of University Associates, for their encouragement, support, and editorial suggestions; Marion Fusco, managing editor at University Associates, for her editorial assistance; Deborah A.

Osborn, an editor at University Associates, for serving as the main editorial supervisor in finalizing the manuscript; Kent D. Beeler, my colleague at Eastern Michigan University, for supporting me in the completion of this project; the many students-learners for offering feedback to the contributors on the affective activities; and my wife, Jeanne, a teacher in the Ypsilanti Public Schools, for helping in all parts of the process—editing, typing, proofreading, and giving me encouragement.

I hope that this book will be a source of new and varied ideas and that readers will feel free to duplicate and modify the strategies for their needs in educational/learning situations.

I would appreciate feedback from those who wish to share information about their experiences with these activities or from those who have other activities with promising potential for use by professionals.

Lou Thayer

Ypsilanti, Michigan
May, 1976

Contents

Introduction

In a time when industrialized society is characterized by an emphasis on material things, facts, and cognitive approaches, it seems imperative to attend to the unmet needs of learners in the affective domain. This book gives special attention to structured experiences that seek to strengthen the affective components of learning: the learners' self-awareness, learning climates, interpersonal relationships in learning, recognition of learner needs and perceptions, and competencies needed for facilitating learning approaches. The focus is on people, their perceptions, and their learning experiences.

The fifty experiences in this book have been developed by people who are involved in humanizing their teaching-learning approaches. The contributors offer a wide variety of educational-learning backgrounds, e.g., all phases of teacher education, psychology, mental health, research education, private and governmental consulting, special education, counseling, counselor education, and student personnel services for higher education. One may wish to write to individual contributors for more information about their work with specific structured experiences. (See the List of Contributors at the end of the book.)

Structured experiences emphasize an experiential learning approach in which the learners are *directly* involved in the process. The participants' feelings, thoughts, and values have a significant place in their personal assimilation of the learning, or meaning, to be derived from the experience.

All the structured experiences in this book have been field tested and, as a result, frequently modified to reflect learner needs. They are designed to be applicable in a wide range of educational-learning settings and levels: elementary, junior high, and secondary schools; undergraduate teacher and psychological education; graduate education in the helping professions of counseling, teaching, social work, etc.; in-service training for teachers, counselors, administrators, and parents; faculty development programs in higher education; personal development seminars; and professional workshops focusing on experiential learning.

1

Regardless of the settings or educational levels, the activities emphasize an experiential approach to learning in which *the focus is on the person*. The participant reflects on his own feelings and perceptions about the experience as he relates cognitive information to his own experiencing. This emphasis on the person holds true even when the structured experiences are applied in strict subject-matter disciplines such as mathematics and physics.

The structured experiences in this book are sequenced with regard to both topical area and complexity. That is, within each topical area, the experiences are arranged from simple activities to more complex ones. As much as possible, the structured experiences are presented as the facilitator (or instructor) might use them over a period of one or more group (class) meetings, a semester, or a year. The topical areas that are of focal interest in this book include the perceptions and development of self; relationships with others; teachers, teaching, and helping processes; learning climates and group processes; feedback techniques; creativity; trust; values-exploration activities; simulations on school and higher education; image recall; and assessment practices.

When selecting a structured experience for a learning situation, it is suggested that the facilitator keep in mind the developmental stage of the group, the participants' needs, and the facilitator's competencies. Particular attention should also be given to the amount of time needed for talking through (processing) the results of the activity. Throughout the total process of selection, implementation, and planning, the facilitator's behavior serves as a model to learners and prospective facilitators. Consequently, it is the facilitator who can bring the structured experience to life and establish it as an experiential approach in which *learning*—not teaching—*is highlighted*. (The following chapter, On Using Structured Experiences, discusses in greater depth the use of structured experiences.)

Each activity has a standard format that includes the goals, group size, time required, physical setting, materials, step-by-step process, variations, notes, and references. Of special interest to the facilitator are the goals, the step-by-step process, and the variations. For example, does the goal meet the purpose for which the structured experience is planned? Can all the steps in the process be exercised accurately and effectively? Is there any need for variations in the original structured experience to meet the goals of the learning group?

A number of the experiences in this handbook include instruments and worksheets, which are designed to be easily reproduced and modified to fit particular learner needs. Also, some structured experiences have specifically prepared stimulus statements for facilitator use, and a number of experiences have homework assignments that can be used to enhance the process.

The designs of these structured experiences can be easily varied to meet the learning needs of different groups. The facilitator is urged to modify these ideas in response to immediate teaching-learning situations. Most of the experiences can be adapted for use with different age levels, with various kinds of learners, and in different educational settings and subject-matter areas.

Suggested readings in affective education are listed in the back of this book. These readings provide excellent sources for ideas and activities that have been used by others.

On Using Structured Experiences

Louis Thayer

Structured experiences can enhance personal growth and the growth of a learning group, whether the setting is a university, a high school, or a place where people have come together for a specific learning objective. The essential goal is a more humanistic approach to the process of learning that focuses on the person and his experiencing rather than on a specific content vehicle. Cognitive material is generally present, but the emphasis is on the affective aspects of learning—the person's feelings, meanings, and perceptions.

Affective education and a humanistic approach are important in my view of the learning process. When I am facilitating, I actively participate in as many structured experiences as possible. My participation has increased the learning about myself, has acquainted me with participants (students) as persons, and has helped to facilitate a more personal learning climate. In this way, students continue to view me as a learner and a person even when I approach the task of facilitation.

When preparing structured experiences, it is important to assess the needs of the learning group. Involving the learners in the planning of the experiences adds significantly to their feeling of ownership regarding the learning outcomes. I prefer those learning experiences in which the participants and I (the facilitator) structure the activities to meet certain group needs. Thus, the experiences conform more with the learners' needs, my own personality, and my teaching-learning style.

I generally prefer to create my own structured experiences or to modify already existing activities. When reviewing an experience prepared by someone else, I view it as a well-organized and tested idea—which can be modified, adapted, revised, rewritten, or developed to suit my needs. There is no obligation to use an experience exactly as it is written.

Structured experiences can be used to meet individual or group needs that often arise during a learning process. But the more spontaneous the use of the structured experience becomes, the more effective it seems to be. Timing in the use of these activities is crucial. Also, the facilitator's competency in selecting and preparing structured experiences with the appropriate complexity is reflected in how effectively

5

the activity meets the learning group's needs. In most aspects of facilitation, the leader serves as a constant model of a facilitator; often, his behavior is the main message. By observing and interacting with the group leader, participants have the opportunity to learn facilitation skills. The facilitator may want to discuss his own behavior and its purpose at different intervals for this type of learning.

Additional points to be considered are some reasons for *not* using the experiences. It is not effective to use structured experiences to solve emotional problems or to "fill" class or group time. Nor is it useful "to see what will happen" or to use them if the facilitator is absent from a session.

The Facilitator

Most of us can identify a person who facilitates personal growth in others and provides stimulating learning climates. For example, think of an acquaintance who has all the qualities to be a good counselor or a facilitator. I suggest that you close your eyes for a few seconds and think about this person. What characteristics describe this person? From reviews of research and my own experiences, I have learned that the effective helper or facilitator has three outstanding personal qualities: genuineness, empathy, and respect for others. Rogers (1965) describes these qualities as *congruence, empathy,* and *unconditional positive regard.*

Rogers (1965) believes that "personal growth is facilitated when the facilitator* is what he *is,* when in the relationship with his client he is genuine and without 'front' or facade, openly being the feelings and attitudes which at that moment are flowing in him" (pp. 50-51). This is congruence or genuineness.

The second quality is empathy. "The facilitator* is experiencing an accurate empathic understanding of his client's private world, and is able to communicate some of the significant fragments of that understanding" (p. 53).

The third quality is the unconditionality of positive regard, or respect for others. "The facilitator* is experiencing a warm, positive, acceptant attitude toward what *is* in the client" (p. 54). In other words, he prizes the participant.

If the facilitator is perceived by the participants as a person and a learner who is striving for genuineness, empathy, and respect for others, he is regarded as an effective leader. These qualities are necessary

---

*The word *facilitator* has been substituted for the term *counselor* in the three quotes from Carl Rogers.

whether one is counseling, teaching-learning in the classroom, or facilitating groups.

When these three qualities become more representative of the total group, they lead to a general climate that highly stimulates interpersonal relationships for the facilitation of learning (Rogers, 1969). I believe that structured experiences cannot be truly effective without these growth conditions. In an understanding, warm, non-evaluative atmosphere, learners share significant thoughts and feelings about themselves—a sharing that leads to greater self-disclosure and risk taking. If the climate is changing in this positive direction, the process becomes more personalized and the *structured* experience is de-emphasized. The process becomes the lesson.

According to Combs' (1969) studies of helping persons, those who were most effective perceived people and their behaviors as friendly, worthy, and helpful; perceived themselves as *with* people, dependable, and wanted; perceived the task of teaching as a freeing, revealing, and an encouraging process; and had a general frame of reference that was internal, toward people, and toward perceptual meanings.

Do you perceive other people and their behavior as friendly/ unfriendly, worthy/unworthy, helpful/hindering? Do you perceive yourself as *with* people/*apart* from people, dependable/undependable, wanted/unwanted? Do you perceive the task of teaching as freeing/ controlling, revealing/concealing, an encouraging process/goal achievement? Is your general frame of reference internal/external, people/things, perceptual meanings/facts and events? Do you want to be in a position to help others grow personally? Do you want to help enough to be in a growing-changing posture yourself? These are just a few questions that can help a facilitator review his own potential effectiveness in helping others.

Clarifying Expectations

Perhaps the most essential ingredient in getting the structured experience off to a positive start is to clarify facilitator and participant expectations. *Participants have a right to expect clarification before the process begins.* It is helpful for the facilitator to discuss the participants' expectations and then to share his own. In that way, discussion, clarification, and perhaps replanning can follow. Above all, honesty is essential. Participants usually expect to hear about the facilitator's competence and qualifications if not known, how the activity fits the planning for their needs, what part they might play in overall planning, any effects on evaluation, what the essence of the facilitator's participation will be, whether there will be sufficient time for all aspects of the experience with no unnecessary abbreviation, and, above all, that their individual rights will be protected and not subjected to unwarranted group pressure.

If for some reason the participants will be subjected to a certain amount of risk or to unknown agenda items, everyone should be informed ahead of time. Facilitators will find that discussions prior to the experience do not compromise the effectiveness of the process. And, occasionally, a person may choose not to participate in part of a structured experience, which is that person's prerogative.

The Structured Experience Process

My use of structured experiences stresses the experiential approach to learning. An attempt is made to *involve* people in experiences rather than to talk about the experiences vicariously. Each person is encouraged to assimilate the events in his own personal, unique way. The participants and the facilitator seek ways in which their here-and-now feelings and thoughts can be shared and related to their total learning processes. Although didactic material is not totally neglected, the emphasis is on the person and his own assimilation of the events. Consequently, I start with the person's perceptions of his own behavior in the activities because these self-perceptions, rather than feedback from others, trigger the true *learning* aspect of the experiences.

Cognitive material can be offered by the facilitator in several ways. Mini-lectures are effective when they are spontaneous, brief, extemporaneous, and based primarily on a sequence of real events that are witnessed or experienced by the learners. The mini-lecture often consists of pulling together or summarizing the evident and not-so-evident principles in the activities and the interactions. Although the mini-lecture usually comes from the facilitator, other members of the group often give excellent presentations, which have a very positive effect on the group climate. More than one person can be viewed as a facilitator and a resource person.

Another way of presenting cognitive material is to use handouts, films, or other materials for dissemination or viewing. These additional methods can be effective if they are introduced at an appropriate time in the group's process. Often, a group may wish to prepare its own handout or a short skit reviewing the activities and the principles learned. Preparing skits that reflect the experiences can be great fun.

Jones and Pfeiffer (1975) have suggested five revolving steps in the experiential model. Each step plays a significant part in the total *learning* strategy for the participants.

Experiencing: The process usually starts with experiencing. The partici-pant becomes involved in an activity; he *acts* or *behaves* in some way or he *does, performs, observes, sees, says* something. This initial experience is the basis for the entire process.

Publishing: Following the experience itself, it becomes important for the participant to share or "publish" his reactions and observations with oth-ers who have either experienced or observed the same activity.

Processing: Sharing one's reactions is only the first step. An essential—and often neglected—part of the cycle is the necessary integration of this shar-ing. The dynamics that emerged in the activity are explored, discussed, and evaluated (processed) with other participants.

Generalizing: Flowing logically from the processing step is the need to de-velop principles or extract generalizations from the experience. Stating learnings in this way can help participants further define, clarify, and elaborate on them.

Applying: The final step in the cycle is to plan applications of the principles derived from the experience. The experiential process is not complete until a new learning or discovery is used and tested behaviorally. This is the "experimental" part of the experiential model. Applying, of course, be-comes an experience in itself, and with new experience, the cycle begins again. (p. 4)

Process Assessment

Process assessment in the structured experience is of equal importance to experiencing as part of the learning strategy. The assessment phase of the total process can be a powerful stimulus to personal behavior changes outside the learning group. There must be ample opportunity for each participant to talk about his feelings and perceptions of the "experiencing" segment (Jones & Pfeiffer, 1975). Improper processing can lead to an aborted learning activity.

Special attention must also be given when nonverbal and fantasy experiences are used. I am very careful not to make any assumptions concerning the thoughts and feelings that are stimulated in such ex-periences. What appears positive to some individuals may prove nega-tive to others. Participants must be helped to assess the experience thoroughly.

Process assessment usually focuses on the experiences and per-ceptions of individuals and the interactions of the group during the ses-sion. Numerous topical areas are possible in the assessment phase: attitudes toward oneself and others, relationships with significant oth-ers, beliefs about people, purposes of learning and growing, changing behaviors "when I go back home," setting goals, etc.

There are several ways of grouping the participants for the assess-ment phase (Thayer, 1973).

Self-assessment: The individual is encouraged to look carefully at himself, his perceptions, his goals, his values, and his behaviors and their effects on others. Often stimulus statements prepared by the facilitator are given to encourage the consideration of specific topics.

One-to-one sharing: Feedback is provided to the participant by an observer (or observers) with an emphasis on exhibited behaviors—both verbal and nonverbal. Having more than one person share this observation with a participant provides for interesting comparisons of the perceptions about a person's behavior and the actual meanings behind these behaviors.

Small-group assessment (eight to fifteen people): The assessment is conducted by the participants and the facilitator after the experiencing segment. The time is used to point out and discuss various individual perceptions and principles of group interaction that were experienced. Occasionally, this is a very opportune time to give appropriate mini-lectures on group process and related topics.

Large-group assessment (fifteen to forty people): When the group is large, opportunities for each individual to review and relate his perceptions are reduced. The facilitator may need to use his leadership skills to encourage discussion of topics and personal perceptions. An alternative is to divide the large group into smaller subgroups for discussion.

Several additional assessment aids can be used in different groupings for assessment (Thayer, 1973):

The expert or panel of observers: The facilitator can share his perceptions about the activity and then call for reactions from the participants. Alternatively, a panel of observers can be selected to represent the general feelings of the larger group.

Group-on-group observation: Small groups can be used to observe another group in process. Members of the observing group may be assigned to monitor different aspects of the other group. They can often discover and discuss principles of group process and learning. A variation of this format, suggested by Gorman (1974), is the use of three groups formed in concentric circles. The inner group is the interacting group. In the middle group, each member carefully observes and takes notes of a specific person's behavior in the interacting group. After a specified amount of time, each member of the inner group has an opportunity to talk to his observer-coach for feedback and help. The process can continue after a short help session. The third group observes and notes for discussion the general processes that focus on principles of group interaction, such as leadership, roles, norms, etc. Observation sheets may be prepared in advance for use with this type of assessment format.

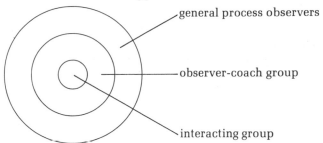

general process observers

observer-coach group

interacting group

Written materials: Stimulus materials, including questions or incomplete sentences, may be used to encourage individuals to review their experiences and perceptions. Other materials might include case studies or anecdotal reports for comparison with group experiences or an extension of the learning format.

Audiotape and/or videotape recording: Recording equipment allows playback of the entire session or selected segments for assessment purposes. These aids can be used in many unique ways; however, they can be very threatening to some individuals. Plans for using recording equipment should be discussed and agreed upon with participants *prior* to the structured experience.

Assignments: The facilitator or instructor may find some optional assignments helpful to learners. The participants may be asked to keep a log of their feelings, thoughts, and the principles learned in the structured experience. They may also be asked to write an assessment of their own perceptions and behaviors in the experience or a critical analysis of the group session describing roles, types of leadership, and other group processes. Some facilitators may utilize this approach to ask for written assessments of their roles as group facilitators.

Imagery: Participants can be asked to close their eyes and to recall actual images of the experience. Usually the facilitator can provide stimulus statements for the participants to visualize certain events. Muscular relaxation facilitates the use of imagery to recall experiences. After the experience has been visualized, participants can be encouraged to discuss any perceptions or feelings they encountered while imaging the previous events.

Fantasy: A short fantasy trip may follow the use of imagery. Participants can fantasize how they would like the experience to have proceeded or how they might use the structured experience in their own work setting. They can develop goals, ways in which they would change behaviors, or ways to transfer new experimental behaviors to everyday life situations.

Helping students integrate the new principles they have learned is an important part of the process. If the learning is to last, participants must be helped to set goals and establish plans for the transfer of their new learnings to everyday relationships—to open avenues for exploring ways to apply their new learnings. The process can be continued to help participants establish plans for behavioral change, experiment with new behaviors, assess their behaviors, and continue experimenting again.

When the total structured experience or the process is genuine and meaningful, participants share very personal feelings, concerns, and perceptions. At appropriate times, I have offered personal assistance in the form of individual and group counseling. However, if the facilitator is not qualified to counsel, he should be able to assist participants in finding other sources of assistance.

Feedback Principles

Although feedback is not a part of the process in every structured experience, the frequency of its use in experiences warrants attention. If feedback is involved in the learning process, the facilitator should spend time discussing principles of feedback, giving examples of each principle, and asking participants to review their own verbal feedback behavior prior to the beginning of the structured experience.

Participants are encouraged to focus more on individual strengths than on weaknesses. This point is crucial in establishing a positive learning climate. My experiences in learning groups have led me to encourage others not to make too many assumptions about people and the reasons for their behavior.

The implementation of an experience is more successful when a positive attitude is expressed by the facilitator. Each person in a learning group can assume responsibility for assisting others in learning, and feedback is one way that people can help each other. Feedback to individuals and the way in which it is provided often affect the learning climate and the beneficial effects experienced by individuals.

Johnson (1972) has prepared eleven principles on the use of feedback.

1. Focus feedback on behavior rather than on persons.
2. Focus feedback on observations rather than on inferences.

3. Focus feedback on description rather than on judgment.
4. Focus feedback on descriptions of behavior which are in terms of "more or less" rather than in terms of "either-or."
5. Focus feedback on behavior related to a specific situation, preferably to the "here-and-now," rather than on behavior in the abstract, placing it in the "there-and-then."
6. Focus feedback on the sharing of ideas and information rather than on giving advice.
7. Focus feedback on exploration of alternatives rather than on answers or solutions.
8. Focus feedback on the value it may have to the receiver, not on the value of "release" that it provides the person giving the feedback.
9. Focus feedback on the amount of information that the person receiving it can use, rather than on the amount that you have which you might like to give.
10. Focus feedback on time and place so that personal data can be shared at appropriate times.
11. Focus feedback on *what* is said rather than *why* it is said.

(pp. 16-17)

A handout listing these principles can be prepared for discussion and used throughout the group process. I find that the principles help almost everyone become more aware of *verbal* and *nonverbal* feedback during the experience.

Modifying a Structured Experience

Implementing an activity according to the original format is especially helpful for facilitators who are only beginning to use structured experiences to reach learning goals or to change to a more humanistic approach. However, by varying parts of a structured experience, the facilitator can add significantly to its overall usefulness in the learning group's setting. It is suggested that the facilitator study carefully the structured experience as it relates to the learning situation before he uses the experience. The facilitator may be able to note the basic area(s) in which a change or variation will need to be made to meet the specific learning objectives in the experiential process.

The process of modifying a structured experience may be most efficiently and systematically carried out by beginning with a comparison of the stated goals of the structured experience and those of the learning group. If the general goal stated matches the desired outcome for the group, then the facilitator can make sure that each segment of the structured experience fits his needs or he can modify the goals, group size, time required, physical setting, materials, or step-by-step process to reach his objectives. Often, other handbooks on structured experiences (e.g., Pfeiffer & Jones, 1973, 1975) offer good ideas for variations with similar theme-oriented structured experiences. As the facilitator uses or develops experiences, he may wish to take notes during the process or let the group brainstorm for new ideas after the experience has ended. Frequently, participants are most helpful in pinpointing process steps that need altering.

Planning and Sequencing

When I use certain activities to facilitate learning groups, I plan the sequence in which I intend to use the structured experiences over the course of the sessions. I generally plan the experiential segment of the learning so that the structured experiences flow from relatively simple to increasingly complex in terms of values, attitudes, and group process. Process assessment, used after each structured experience, affects the content and direction of future experiences. As much as possible, I share the responsibility for planning future activities with the participants (students). The participants usually feel good about being able to modify the process.

Conclusion

If structured experiences are successful and good group learning conditions develop, groups tend to move away from the need for structure to approach certain topics, values, and behaviors. The focus is on more personal, human interaction and learning. With honesty, trust, understanding, and positive regard, threat to individuals is at a minimum. The facilitator also becomes a participant and can experience controversial topics, complex value systems, and interpersonal relationships. So, in a way, structured experiences can be used successively to approximate a situation or an environment in which no formal structure is needed. Persons come together to learn what they wish to learn. I find that this trend away from structure happens somewhat naturally if most participants, including the facilitator, are genuinely seeking *to become more of the persons they can be.* That's exciting.

References

Combs, A. W. *Florida studies in the helping professions.* Gainesville: University of Florida Press, 1969. Social Sciences Monograph No. 37.

Gorman, A. *Teachers and learners: The interactive process* (2nd ed.). Boston: Allyn & Bacon, 1974.

Johnson, D. *Reaching out: Interpersonal effectiveness and self-actualization.* Englewood Cliffs, N.J.: Prentice-Hall, 1972.

Jones, J. E., & Pfeiffer, J. W. (Eds.). *The 1975 annual handbook for group facilitators.* La Jolla, Calif.: University Associates, 1975.

Pfeiffer, J. W., & Jones, J. E. (Eds.). *A handbook of structured experiences for human relations training* (Vols. IV & V). La Jolla, Calif.: University Associates, 1973, 1975.

Rogers, C. R. *Freedom to learn.* Columbus, Ohio: Charles E. Merrill, 1969.

Rogers, C. R. The interpersonal relationship: The core of guidance. In R. L. Mosher, R. F. Carle, & C. D. Kehas (Eds.), *Guidance: An examination.* New York: Harcourt, Brace & World, 1965.

Thayer, L. C. Process assessment as a learning strategy. A paper delivered at the American Educational Research Association's Annual Convention, The Special Interest Group: Affective Aspects of Education, New Orleans, March 1973.

1

A Person with Heart: Becoming Acquainted

Louis Thayer

Goals

I. To help people become better acquainted by sharing their thoughts and feelings about a symbolic design.

II. To identify personal qualities that individuals wish to strengthen or develop.

Group Size

Small groups of six to eight people.

Time Required

Approximately thirty to forty minutes.

Physical Setting

A room large enough to accommodate the groups. Comfortable seating is preferred.

Materials

I. A copy of this book with the design of the "symbolic man," or a copy of the cover design, for each participant.

II. Paper and pencils.

de Passillé/Sylvestre

Step-by-Step Process

    I. The facilitator distributes the symbolic designs and paper and pencils to each group. He asks the participants to study the design of the symbolic man, noting on paper their first reactions and the meaning the design holds for them. (Four to five minutes.)

    II. The members of each group share their reactions to the design, relating only the reactions and perceptions that they feel comfortable in sharing. (Seven to ten minutes.)

    III. After the first round of sharing, the facilitator asks the participants to think of a person in their lives who has (or had) "heart." He may need to explain what is meant by "heart"—someone who has a zest for life, is helpful to others, cares about people, meets life's challenges, is a model for others, etc.

    IV. When the participants have a person in mind, the facilitator asks them to:
      1. List the personal qualities of this person;
      2. Note which of these qualities the participants also possess;
      3. Note which qualities the participants wish to strengthen or develop in themselves.

    V. Each participant is asked to describe briefly the person he feels has "heart" and some of the personal qualities of that person. (Approximately two minutes for each participant.)

    VI. The members of each group share one personal quality that they feel is a strength of theirs. (One minute for each participant.)

    VII. The participants share one personal quality that they wish to strengthen or develop in themselves. (One minute for each participant.)

    VIII. Focusing on one person at a time, each group offers some positive feedback to the group members on the way in which they are perceived. (Two to three minutes for each participant.) Everyone is encouraged to contribute a response when each person is highlighted.

    IX. The facilitator leads a general discussion with all the groups on the "symbolic man," the persons they chose who had "heart," and where they might be in terms of personal development.

Variations

   I. Between steps III and IV, the participants may be asked to indicate how the cover design could be altered or modified to be more representative of a person with "heart."

  II. The facilitator may wish to substitute a different symbolic design or let the participants select their own pictures for use in the process.

2

What's in a Name?: Expanding Awareness

Stuart N. Hart

Goals

I. To expand awareness of the influences of names, of the ways in which they are used, and of the many effects that they may have on the perceptions, behaviors, and opportunities of individuals.

II. To explore how people use names in ways that influence their interaction with others.

III. To discover how each participant feels about his own name (emphasis on first name) and how his perceptions have influenced his own development, opportunities, and relationships.

Group Size

Preferably eight to twelve people, although the activity is also effective with more participants.

Time Required

Approximately fifty minutes.

Physical Setting

A large room with chairs arranged in a circle to promote more eye contact.

Materials

I. A name tag for each participant. (The name should be large enough to be read easily.)

II. Felt-tipped markers.

Step-by-Step Process

    I. The facilitator asks the participants to form a circle and to place name tags on themselves.

    II. The facilitator introduces the goals of the activity and offers an example of how names influence people, e.g., classroom seating and the ease in remembering names. He suggests that thinking about and discussing names may be a good way to get to know each other better as well as to consider how names influence people.

    III. Each participant is encouraged to share with the group his knowledge of his name's origin, how it was selected, his nicknames, and the attitudes he and others have held toward the name. He also shares any influences, advantages, or disadvantages that he feels his name has had on his life and whether or not he would prefer another name. The facilitator joins in this process or models the process in a genuine manner.

    IV. The facilitator assists the participants in reviewing various aspects about names, e.g.,
      1. Historical origins or definitions;
      2. How and why a name is chosen by the parents;
      3. Nicknames;
      4. Attitudes people have held or expressed toward names;
      5. Influences, advantages, or disadvantages that names may have had on the participants;
      6. Whether or not the participants would prefer to have another name and, if so, which one and why;
      7. What participants would name or have named their own children.

    V. The facilitator focuses the group on becoming more sensitive to other people's names, remembering names, and noticing how communication is affected by the use of names.

Variations

    I. The facilitator may wish to discuss the following uses of names.
      1. How names and name-title combinations are used to denote social and professional distance. For example, a principal and his teachers may refer to each other by first name, title and last name, or a combination of both.
      2. How names and name-title combinations are used to clarify authority-responsibility relationships and relative positions of maturity. For example, the boss is called Mr. Smith and the younger employee is called Sam.

3. How name forms are used to indicate whether communication is warm or cold; rigid or flexible; accepting, directing, or rejecting. For example, consider the difference between having a mother call her son "Jimmy" versus "James Lee Thorpe!"

4. How names with a recognizable ethnic, family, or personal history may elicit positive and/or negative prejudiced behavior.

5. How some names have unisex appeal; for example, Jean-Gene, Francis-Frances, Billie-Billy, Marian-Marion.

6. How elimination of last names might be consistent with existential and other supports for emphasizing the individual uniqueness, rights, and responsibilities of each person.

7. How some names may lead to self-fulfilling prophecies; for example, Rocco, shortened to Rock (tough, aggressive male).

8. How some individuals have little more than the recognition and proper pronunciation of their names by others to indicate that they exist and are of importance to others; for example, the disadvantaged student who becomes belligerent and hostile when his name is mispronounced.

9. How teachers can influence the educational, personal, and social development of their students by the manner in which they use names and allow or encourage students to use theirs; for example, seating of students; two-way, first-name communication; last name or title and name relationship or double standard; calling on and encouraging students whose names can be remembered more often than those whose names cannot.

10. How each person may partially choose and express the levels and types of relationships he wants by what he calls others and encourages others to call him.

II. The facilitator may also wish to examine the relationships between the names of past acquaintances or famous people and a person's present perceptions of those names and of people who have those names.

3

Public Versus Private Self:
Self-Disclosure

Kent D. Beeler

Goals

I. To enable the group members to become better acquainted by sharing personal information that they would not normally volunteer.

II. To focus the participants' attention on feelings and thoughts related to disclosing their public and private selves.

Group Size

A large group that can be divided into several small groups of four persons each.

Time Required

Two group sessions: one for task assignment (ten minutes) and another for the sharing process (forty minutes).

Physical Setting

Any room in which the learning group meets.

Materials

I. A 4" x 6" index card for each participant.

II. Felt-tipped markers.

III. Pencils.

IV. Masking tape (optional).

Step-by-Step Process

I. The facilitator assigns each participant the task of writing a statement about his public and his private self. He distributes the index

23

cards and markers and explains how the statements should be prepared. Each description should contain no more than twenty-five words; only descriptive words and phrases should be used.

II. The participants are asked to fold the index cards and to label the outside public self and the inside private self.

The participants are asked to prepare the statements at home for the next group meeting.

III. At the next group meeting, the facilitator divides the participants into several small groups of four persons each. Each participant is asked to share information about his public self with his group.

IV. After this sharing process, the facilitator encourages the participants to share some comments about their private selves.

V. The facilitator asks the participants in each group to discuss how they felt while they prepared the statements and while they shared them with the group. (The focus is on self-disclosure.) He distributes pencils and asks the participants to write these feelings on the back of their cards for review later in the session.

VI. The facilitator asks each group to note things that hinder and help self-disclosure of a personal nature. The discussion may include past experiences with self-disclosure.

VII. The large group reconvenes to discuss the advantages and disadvantages of disclosing information of a personal nature. The facilitator emphasizes the resources, ideas, and feelings generated by learning about one's peers. The participants may wish to post their statements in a public place, such as on a bulletin board.

Variations

I. The participants can be encouraged to review and revise their statements at the end of the first group session and to continue sharing in small groups or in the large group.

II. Written assignments can be made on the topic of self-disclosure and personal experiences. Arguments may be presented on the positive aspects of disclosing oneself and the negative points of too much personal sharing. The conditions, process, outcomes, and persons involved are points on which to dwell.

III. The participants can complete their public and private statements at the beginning of the session, thereby eliminating the homework assignment.

Reference

Mathis, B. C., & McGaghie, W. C. (Eds.). *Profiles in college teaching: Models at Northwestern.* Evanston, Ill.: The Center for the Teaching Professions, Northwestern University, 1972.

4

Personal Collage: A Focus on Feelings

Edward W. Schultz

Goals

I. To increase the participants' awareness of their feelings.

II. To heighten awareness of similarities and differences in the participants' feelings.

III. To encourage self-disclosure in a group setting.

Group Size

Up to twenty-five participants. The activity works well with elementary and junior high school students.

Time Required

The activity is most effective if conducted on five consecutive days (approximately thirty minutes each day for four days and a longer session on the fifth day).

Physical Setting

A classroom or a lounge area with a large table on which the materials can be placed.

Materials

I. One large piece of poster board for each participant.

II. A large supply of magazines and newspapers.

III. Several pair of scissors and bottles of glue.

IV. Shellac and brushes (optional).

Step-by-Step Process

I. The facilitator explains that each participant will select a picture from a magazine or a newspaper that reflects his general feeling or frame of mind on this particular day. The same process will be repeated for each of the next four days so that at the end of the week, each participant will have accumulated five pictures. A group discussion will follow each selection process to share thoughts and feelings about the pictures. Afterward, each participant will glue his picture to a piece of poster board, which represents his own personal collage.

II. The participants are allowed fifteen minutes to choose pictures that reflect their feelings and emotions for the day. The pictures should be cut carefully so that they can be glued to the poster boards later in the session.

III. The facilitator assembles the group members in a circle to share comments about the pictures. Each participant is encouraged to share his picture and to indicate how it reflects his feelings and what it symbolizes to him.

IV. The facilitator assists the participants in discussing their feelings and points toward the similarities and dissimilarities among group members' feelings. He may ask the group to record a list of words used to express feelings.

V. After the group discussion, the facilitator distributes the poster board that will be used for the participants' personal collages. Each group member glues his picture to his own piece of poster board. The boards are safely stored for the next group meeting.

VI. Steps II through V are repeated for the next three days.

VII. On the final (fifth) day, step II is repeated. Then each participant glues his final picture to his personal collage to prepare for the group discussion. During the sharing process, each person reviews his last picture and his entire personal collage and summarizes briefly his feelings for the week. The following questions may be discussed.
   1. What were the predominant feelings?
   2. How many different feelings were presented?
   3. How difficult was it to disclose feelings to the group?
   4. How did the participants' feelings affect their learning or school work?
   Other stimulus questions may also be presented.

VIII. The facilitator focuses the discussion on the causes of both positive and negative feelings. Some caution is advised if recent events are especially traumatic to participants, e.g., severe family problems, a death in the family.

IX. The discussion continues, focusing on what causes different feelings and what can be done about their effects. After the discussion, the facilitator may assist the participants in shellacking their personal collages.

Variations

I. If the activity is conducted with elementary school students, the facilitator may ask them to learn how to spell the "feeling" words. At the end of each of the first four sessions, a spelling lesson can be generated; a quiz can be given on the fifth day.

II. The participants may be assigned a descriptive writing exercise in which they prepare a short statement describing their pictures and their feelings.

III. A group collage expressing "feelings" about a topic or a situation can be generated instead of individual collages.

5

The Last Paper: A Review of Personal Learning*

Louis Thayer

Goal

To encourage the participants to review and assess major learnings and directions in their lives.

Group Size

Any number of participants.

Time Required

To be completed during a semester—usually over a period of three to four months.

Materials

Paper and pencils.

Step-by-Step Process

I. The facilitator describes the project to the learning group, emphasizing that the assignment should be undertaken strictly on a voluntary basis.

II. The facilitator relates the following expectations concerning the task:
1. Do not attempt the assignment unless you can devote an appropriate amount of time and energy to introspection.
2. The paper can be any length you desire.
3. The paper need not be handed in as long as the instructor knows that it has been completed or is still in progress.

---

*From "Assignment: The Last Paper," by L. C. Thayer, *New Directions in Teaching,* 1975, 5(1), 41-42. Copyright © 1975 by Office of Experimental Studies, Bowling Green State University, Bowling Green, Ohio. Adapted and reprinted by permission.

4. You must be able to trust the instructor *if you choose* to allow him to read your paper.
5. The instructor will take the time to read, react to, and discuss your paper with you, if you wish.
6. The paper will not be evaluated and will affect your grade in the course only insofar as it is a part of a contractual arrangement.
7. It is beneficial to select at least one significant person whom you trust and with whom you will share the final paper. After that person reads your paper, ask him to write some comments or share some perceptions about you and your paper.
8. You may wish to save your paper for future reading, planning, and possible revision.

III. The facilitator provides the following stimulus statement for each person who voluntarily chooses to undertake the project. Absolutely no instructor judgment or evaluation accompanies the task.

If for some unknown reason this were to be the last paper you would ever write, try to write a paper in which a person could come to know you personally and gain a clearer understanding of you, your philosophy of life, your directions (goals) in living, and the significant learnings in life affecting you. When you are preparing this paper, try to give consideration to the following questions:
How have I come to think the thoughts I have?
How have I come to be the person I am?
How can I become the person I want to be?

IV. If necessary, arrangements must be made by the facilitator for the application of the project toward a course requirement or a grade. Dates for completion of the paper must also be set.

V. When an individual has completed the paper, a time may be scheduled for the instructor and the person to review the paper and the process *if the person has decided to request the facilitator to read the final paper.*

Variations

I. Some participants may wish to complete this project with the aid of an audiotape recorder. The final essay may be an edited version of several audiotape recordings.

II. The facilitator can select less personal topical themes and have the learning group participants prepare a paper on all their learnings from experiences in that area.

Reference

Rogers, C. R. *On becoming a person*. Boston: Houghton Mifflin, 1961.

6

My Life:
An Awareness of Self

Judith A. Redwine

Goal

To help the participants become more aware of the internal controls that govern their lives.

Group Size

Any size learning group.

Time Required

Schedules for completion of the task should be arranged between the facilitator and each writer.

Physical Setting

Any room in which the learning group meets.

Materials

Each individual can choose his own unique way of presenting his autobiographical sketch, e.g., slides, audiotapes, a book of drawings, a book of poems.

Step-by-Step Process

I. The facilitator introduces the assignment of the autobiographical sketch, which is to be completed throughout the course of the group meetings. He announces that the task is strictly voluntary and affects any evaluation only by contractual arrangement since the sketch may or may not be examined by him.

II. The facilitator explains that at certain points during the learning group process, the focus of each of the five chapters in the autobiographical sketch will be introduced, at which time the learning group will hold a full-scale discussion on the topic.

III. The facilitator assigns the topical focus of the first chapter. (See the Autobiographical Task Sheet.) Several stimulus statements are used for the general discussion and then given as aids only for the writers. The participants may wish to take extensive notes during the discussion.

IV. The learning group and the facilitator decide whether the chapters will be presented and/or discussed at the completion of each chapter or when all chapters have been finished. *Any person may choose not to present all or selected parts of his sketch.*

V. At appropriate times during the remainder of the learning group process, the facilitator assigns the other four chapters and holds in-depth discussions on each topic.

VI. After all chapters have been completed, the facilitator asks the individuals to prepare a one-page summary of each chapter that reflects any significant learnings derived from doing the task.

VII. The facilitator discusses ways in which the materials and/or significant learnings in the sketches may be processed. Trust, openness, empathy, risk, acceptance, genuineness, confidentiality, and disclosure may be considered.

Variations

I. If time allows, the sketches could be processed with the facilitator or a trusted friend. Again, sharing within the group can take place after each completed chapter or when all five chapters are completed.

II. The facilitator and the group members may choose to alter the topical focus of the chapter and write their own stimulus statements.

III. Arrangements can be made for the writers to share particular sections or chapters of their sketches with other group members.

IV. The class may be asked to write bumper-sticker quotes that relate a personal philosophy. This could be an activity apart from the autobiographical sketch.

Reference

Keen, S. *To a dancing god.* New York: Harper & Row, 1970.

AUTOBIOGRAPHICAL TASK SHEET

Chapter 1—How Have I Become the Person I Am?

Who were the most important people that you admired? What were the crucial decisions for which you were responsible? What hurts do you resent having suffered? What gifts were you given for which you are grateful?

Chapter 2—Living in the Present Moment

How do you feel about yourself at this moment in time/space? How do you feel about significant people around you? If you were to make a bumper sticker that expresses you to the world, what would it say? What makes you happy now? What makes you unhappy?

Chapter 3—Future Fantasy

If you could *do, have,* or *be* anything you wanted in your wildest dreams, what kind of future would you invent for yourself?

Chapter 4—Real Future

If everything goes rather well for you, how will things be in ten years? What will you be doing? What will you be feeling? Where will you be living? What things will you have? With what kind of people will you be associated? Relationships? In twenty years?

Chapter 5—Death with Dignity

How and when will you die? What is it that abides, that is not conquered by death? How do thoughts of death affect your living? Write your eulogy.

7

Favorite Passages: Personal Interpretations

Kent D. Beeler

Goals

   I. To provide an opportunity for the group members to share a selected passage (statement, lyric, quotation, poem, etc.) that holds special meaning and significance for them.

  II. To discover how the passages have affected the participants' attitudes and behavior.

 III. To emphasize the need to understand the differences between individual experiences.

Group Size

Small groups of six to eight persons each.

Time Required

Approximately five to seven minutes per person if group discussion follows the passage. The activity should be assigned to the participants one group meeting prior to its intended use.

Physical Setting

Any informal group setting.

Materials

   I. A 4" x 6" index card for each participant.

  II. Audio-visual equipment may be needed if some individuals have selected slides, records, or audiotapes to present their passages.

Step-by-Step Process

   I. One group session prior to the use of the passages, the facilitator asks each participant to bring to class a favorite passage that holds special meaning and significance. The passage should be typed or neatly printed on a 4″ x 6″ card provided by the facilitator.

II. At the next session, the facilitator divides the participants into small groups and asks each person to share as many of the following steps as he feels comfortable in revealing.

1. Relate your favorite passage and provide a brief explanation of the meaning and special significance of the passage.

2. Verbalize how you came into contact with the passage, making use of any related incident or experience, e.g., the circumstances (place, people), your emotional state at that time, any change in feelings that accompanied the finding of the passage.

3. Describe how the passage might hold significance for others.

4. Allow group members to respond and share experiences related to the commentary.

III. The facilitator reassembles the large group and initiates a discussion on the need to recognize differences and meanings in the experiences of individuals.

Variations

I. The facilitator can select several passages with related themes or topical focus for discussion in step III.

II. Before dividing the large group into smaller groups, the facilitator may wish to share his favorite passage with the large group. It is also effective for the facilitator to participate as a contributor in one of the groups.

III. The participants may be expected to write a one-page commentary on their passages for homework.

IV. A bulletin-board display can be made with the favorite passages.

V. Small groups can develop a short skit around a special passage to be enacted before the large group. This variation could easily follow step II in the structured experience.

VI. Symbolic designs or word pictures can be used in lieu of passages.

8

Personal Message: An Audiotape Presentation

Leslie Pettis and Louis Thayer

Goal

To provide an individual with the opportunity to prepare and present a personal message about a specific topic.

Group Size

Any size learning group.

Materials

I. Records or audiotapes containing songs and speeches (to be recorded).

II. Blank audiotape, an audiotape recorder, audiotape playback equipment, and a stereo set.

III. Copies of the final bibliography for distribution to the learning group.

Step-by-Step Process

I. The facilitator describes the project to the group and indicates how the audiotape will be utilized.

II. The facilitator outlines some helpful hints about preparing a personal message for presentation and suggests several topics, e.g., war in the Far East or the Middle East, love and peace, death, education, the economy, religion, refugees. He makes the following suggestions for using the audiotape:

1. Decide on a topic or a theme of personal interest for development and presentation to the group.

2. Determine the approximate length of the audiotape desired.

3. Check resource materials for lists of songs, speeches, newspaper clippings, etc., pertaining to the selected topic. The audio portion of radio and television news or excerpts from interviews that the participant has conducted might be used.

4. Listen to and select the excerpts from selected materials to develop the personal theme.
5. Outline the order in which your personal thoughts and materials are to be recorded.
6. Record (edit) on audiotape the selections from songs, speeches, personal thoughts, and other materials.
7. Prepare a bibliography on the materials used in the final audiotape for distribution to the learning group.

III. The facilitator and the individual preparing the audiotape select an appropriate time to present the personal message to the learning group.

IV. At the specified time, each presenter introduces his audiotape project and then plays the audiotape for the learning group. The bibliography should be distributed prior to playing the audiotape.

V. The presenter leads the learning group in a discussion about the personal message on the audiotape. The facilitator joins the group as a participant-observer and also notes for later feedback the various reactions of other participants to the topical theme and the presenter.

VI. The facilitator gives constructive feedback to the presenters and the learning group members about their reactions to the personal message. Every attempt is made to make this a *positive* experience for the presenter.

VII. When the feedback process ends, the group brainstorms for other interesting topics, processes, and materials that might be used for similar experiences.

Variations

I. During the discussion in step V, the facilitator may wish to ask several group members to observe other members interacting with the presenter. They can be involved in the feedback process.

II. With the group's consent, teams may be formed to present opposing personal views or philosophies.

III. Other media may also be used in the presentations, such as slides, pictures, videotape, skits, or even participant-made films.

Notes

The audience can more easily recognize the personal messages of the producers if easily identifiable, contemporary songs, speeches, and artists are used.

9

Bagging Your Needs: Understanding Others

Martin H. Crowe and Gary F. Render

Goals

    I. To demonstrate the relevance of Maslow's Need Hierarchy on the actions of any learning group.

    II. To help each participant identify his own level of need according to the chart and share his feelings about his actions with other group members.

    III. To help each participant examine a common school/learning experience and match it with Maslow's need levels.

Group Size

An already existing class or any learning group.

Time Required

Approximately fifty-five minutes.

Physical Setting

A comfortable room.

Materials

Chalkboard, chalk, and a beanbag.

Step-by-Step Process

    I. The facilitator draws Maslow's hierarchy of human needs on the chalkboard before the group arrives. (See next page.)

    II. When the group's attention is focused on the facilitator, he throws the beanbag at someone in the group.

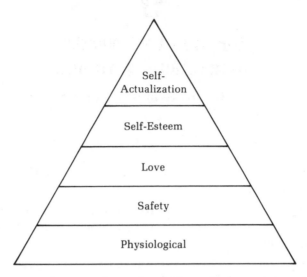

Maslow's Need Hierarchy

III. The facilitator waits to see what happens to the beanbag, avoiding conversation about it as long as possible, even to the point of looking away when directly questioned.

IV. After tensions and strain are very noticeable, the facilitator begins a probing, questioning technique, asking specific persons such questions as: How did you feel when I threw the beanbag? What did you feel when no one threw the bag to you? Were you anxious about holding it? Did you feel group pressure to keep it moving? What were your reasons for throwing it to me? Why didn't you just keep it?

V. Inevitably, someone notices the similarities between the group's feelings and needs and Maslow's hierarchical chart, usually in the areas of safety and belonging. If no one notices, the facilitator encourages discussion in this direction.

VI. The facilitator helps the participants perceive the numerous variations in people's needs, feelings, and motivations even though they share the same experience.

VII. Then the facilitator asks each person to recall another situation or school experience in which he wishes to assess his needs, feelings, and motivations. This examination of other experiences is conducted for as long as there are time and commitment to the task.

Variations

I. This activity can be used as (1) a teaching tool for Maslow's Need Hierarchy, (2) an ice-breaker for group discussions, (3) a learning device to explore group processes, or (4) a learning device to display inconsistencies among thoughts, feelings, and public actions.

II. Because the beanbag will usually return to the facilitator or teacher, the point can be raised as to why responsibility is returned to the leader. The experience is particularly useful in teacher education classes because of the emphasis on student and teacher motivation, feelings, and needs.

III. Instead of utilizing a probing-questioning technique in step IV, the facilitator may wish to respond empathically to people's feelings and discussion of needs. Many more feelings may surface in a more understanding, listening approach.

IV. Rather than continuing with step VII, the facilitator may wish to assign as homework an analysis of a school situation in terms of student feelings, behaviors, needs, and motivations.

Reference

Maslow, A. H. *Motivation and personality* (2nd ed.). New York: Harper & Row, 1970.

10

Your Kind of People: Social Preferences

Ajit K. Das

Goals

I. To help the participants become aware of their social preferences (i.e., the kinds of people they like) and the feelings that they have when their perceptions of others have been either confirmed or not confirmed.

II. To encourage the participants to recognize their feelings when their self-perception has been either confirmed or not confirmed by another person.

III. To foster awareness of how the participants relate to others who do not conform to their stereotyped preferences.

Group Size

Dyads formed from an intermediate-size group of twenty to thirty people. (The facilitator should participate in this dyadic encounter.)

Time Required

One and one-half hours.

Physical Setting

A carpeted room with chairs.

Materials

Paper and pencils.

Step-by-Step Process

I. The facilitator distributes pencils and paper and asks the participants to write a few words or short phrases describing the characteristics of the people that they like, e.g., beautiful, strong, intelligent, rich.

II. The facilitator asks the participants to look around the room to see if they can find someone in the group who fits that description. He instructs the participants to walk up to that person and introduce themselves.

III. Each participant asks his partner to describe how he sees himself. The participant checks the closeness of his perceptions to those of the other person's self-perception.

IV. The participant shares his own perceptions of his partner and his feelings about being "right" or "wrong."

V. Then the participant asks his partner to share his feelings about having his self-perception "confirmed" or "not confirmed."

VI. The facilitator asks the members of each dyad to share with each other how they felt about the encounter, e.g., comfortable/uncomfortable, pleasant/unpleasant, surprised/not surprised.

VII. The facilitator instructs the participants to change partners and to repeat steps III through VI with their new partner. The facilitator gives directions again when needed.

VIII. After two or three dyadic encounters have been experienced by the participants, the facilitator leads a discussion with the entire group in which he shares his experience in one of the encounters. Discussion then focuses on social preferences, accuracy in social perceptions, the need to refrain from making too many assumptions, and relating with those who do not conform to stereotyped perceptions.

Variations

I. This structured experience may be followed by an activity that works on the development of and accuracy in making perceptions about people.

II. This activity may be used for getting-acquainted purposes in large groups. The time for steps II through VI can be cut down considerably.

III. A small-group format could be used instead of dyads by having each group relate to one person at a time.

11

Knowing Your Peers: Developing Friendships

Louis Thayer

Goal

To encourage the participants to develop more friendships by sharing learning experiences.

Group Size

Unlimited.

Time Required

Approximately fifteen to twenty minutes.

Physical Setting

Any classroom in which the learning group regularly meets.

Materials

Paper and pencils.

Step-by-Step Process

I. The facilitator distributes paper and pencils and asks the participants to close their eyes and to picture in their minds as many of the other group members as possible. Then the group members write down all the names of the people whom they imaged. The facilitator participates in the recall process and in all the following steps.

II. The facilitator tells the participants to look around the room and to continue listing as many names of group members as they can remember.

III. He requests that the participants write a short phrase or a word describing some special encounter or impression relating to each name on the list.

IV. The facilitator then directs the participants to mill about the room for several minutes, talking to group members whom they had on their list. (Usually these are people with whom they are most acquainted.) The facilitator encourages all the participants to relate the special impressions of others who were noted on their lists, to use the names of peers when they are interacting with them, and to remember faces, names, and impressions.

V. The facilitator asks the members to continue the interaction by talking to persons with whom they are least acquainted or whose names did not appear on their lists. (Allow several minutes for this step.)

VI. The facilitator suggests that the participants spend the next few minutes seeking out those friends and new acquaintances with whom they would like to continue to share educational, philosophical, or personal thoughts in greater depth.

VII. The facilitator recommends that the process continue at a local bar or a restaurant.

Variations

I. In step VI, the facilitator may wish to pursue a discussion on the values of developing peer relationships in a learning group, the difficulties involved in developing lasting relationships, or meeting and making friends.

II. A sociometric diagram could be constructed on the chalkboard showing the people who are known well and those who are not known as well.

III. In step V, the participants may be encouraged to learn something about those people with whom they are least acquainted.

Notes

Often students complete training programs without knowing many people. Learning is facilitated when one can share ideas with a number of people during that training period. This activity may be done any time during the group sessions. An ideal time for the activity is midway through the learning schedule.

12

A Dyadic Encounter on Teaching

Vincent Peterson

Goals

I. To help present and prospective teachers examine and express their teaching philosophy in a nonthreatening, non-evaluative setting.

II. To encourage openness in sharing ideas, strengths, weaknesses, desires, and fears about the teaching field.

III. To strengthen listening skills, with a special focus on empathic understanding.

IV. To provide a nonthreatening atmosphere for giving and receiving feedback.

Group Size

Any number of dyads.

Time Required

A minimum of ninety minutes. This encounter is most successful if the participants in the dyads have time to complete the entire booklet together. Therefore, every effort should be made to minimize time pressures.

Physical Setting

A quiet, undisturbed, comfortable location in which each dyad can sit facing each other.

Materials

One Dyadic Encounter on Teaching Booklet for each participant. The booklet should be prepared so that each stimulus statement or guideline appears on a separate page. The areas separated by a dotted line and page number indicate the material to be placed on each page of the booklet.

Step-by-Step Process

I. The facilitator informs the participants that each person will have an opportunity to share with another person his feelings and ideas about the field of teaching.

II. The participants pair up with another person. If teachers and prospective teachers are in the group, they may be encouraged to form dyads together. Each dyad receives two copies of the Dyadic Encounter on Teaching Booklet.

III. The facilitator discusses the time limitations and asks the dyads to begin the dyadic encounter by following the guidelines in the booklet. (The facilitator participates as a member of a dyad.)

IV. After the sharing has been completed, the facilitator reassembles the large group. He encourages the participants to share their learnings, to examine additional questions about teaching, and to review the uses and misuses of listening skills and feedback.

Variations

I. A "mini" dyadic encounter may be prepared by deleting some of the stimulus statements.

II. The facilitator may wish to alter several statements in the booklet to correspond with the group's learning situation.

III. The booklet may be used effectively as a discussion guide in a small group of six to eight participants. The practice steps on listening and feedback may be very essential parts for the development of a small-group discussion process.

IV. The dyadic encounter may be divided into two group sessions.

V. The practice steps on listening and feedback may be expanded into larger skill-training group segments.

VI. The stimulus statements may be used in a variety of ways, such as questions to be answered in a self-analysis paper, questions for use in interviewing a full-time teacher, questions to be answered in preparation for a job interview, and statements to be used in raising personal thoughts and questions about teaching as a career.

Reference

Jones, J. E., & Jones, J. J. Dyadic encounter: A program for developing relationships. In J. W. Pfeiffer and J. E. Jones (Eds.), *A handbook of structured experiences for human relations training* (Vol. I). La Jolla, Calif.: University Associates, 1969 & 1974, pp. 97-107.

A DYADIC ENCOUNTER ON TEACHING
Vincent Peterson

1

Read silently. Do not look ahead in this booklet.

Teaching has been described as a lonely profession, in which practitioners "do their own thing" with little if any contact with other practitioners on a professional level. Faculty lounge interaction tends to be superficial at best, and teachers' meetings deal primarily with day-to-day administrative details rather than with basic educational issues. This dyadic encounter experience is designed to facilitate the sharing of educational ideas on a fairly deep level.

2

Sharing ideas successfully with one another involves some basic skills and attitudes. The basic dimensions of a deep sharing relationship are self-awareness, self-disclosure, trust, risk taking, empathic understanding, nonpossessive caring, acceptance, and feedback. In an understanding, warm, non-evaluative atmosphere, an individual confides significant information about himself to someone else, who reciprocates—disclosing himself. This "stretching" results in a greater feeling of trust, understanding, and acceptance, and the relationship becomes closer, allowing more significant self-disclosure and greater risk taking. As you continue to share your ideas and experiences authentically you should come to know and trust each other in ways that may enable you to become highly resourceful to each other.

Note the ground rules for this experience:

1. You should be comfortably seated, directly facing your partner, in a location that is free from distractions. If these conditions are not met, find another setting before proceeding any further.
2. Do not look ahead in the booklet.
3. *All the information discussed is strictly confidential.*
4. Each partner responds to each statement before continuing.
5. The statements are to be completed in the order in which they appear. Do not skip items.
6. The discussion items are open-ended statements and can be completed in whatever depth you wish. You may decline to answer any question simply by telling your partner that you choose not to respond.
7. Either partner can stop the exchange if he becomes obviously uncomfortable or anxious.

Look up. If your partner has finished reading, turn the page and begin.

The name I like to go by is . . .

My teaching experience includes . . .

I teach because . . .

I believe I (am) (am not) an effective teacher because . . .

My primary objectives as a teacher are . . .

I have evidence that I am meeting my objectives from . . .

10

Read through first.

I am (very) (reasonably) (not very) satisfied with the evidence that my students are meeting my objectives.

11

Read through first.

One of the most important skills in getting to know another person is listening (empathic understanding). In order to test your ability to understand what your partner is communicating, both of you should go through the following steps, one at a time:
1. Decide which one of you is to speak first in this unit.
2. The first speaker is to complete the following item in two or three sentences: "When I think about my future as a teacher, I see myself . . ."
3. The second speaker repeats *in his own words* what the first speaker has just said. The first speaker must be satisfied that he has been heard accurately.
4. The second speaker then completes the same item himself in two or three sentences.
5. The first speaker paraphrases what the second speaker just said, to the satisfaction of the second speaker.
6. Share what you have learned about yourself as a listener with your partner. To check the accuracy of your listening and understanding, you may find yourselves saying to each other: "What I hear you saying is . . ."

12

As a teacher, I know that I am helping my students learn to . . .

13

Some negative things students learn in my class are . . .

14

The reasons that I use these methods are . . .

15

The primary way that I test my students is . . .

16

The reason I use this type of testing procedure is . . .

Listening check: "What I hear you saying is . . ."

17

The way I grade is . . .

18

The reason I use this form of grading procedure is . . .

(If your answer is "school policy," can you document that this is your only alternative and also document, using actual cases, what happens to those who deviate from the policy?)

19

The primary way in which I use textbooks is . . .

20

The way in which I use supplementary books and materials is . . .

21

The way in which I deal with emotional problems in the classroom is . . .

22

These questions . . .

23

Principals . . .

24

The reason I teach the things I do is . . .

(If your answer is "school policy," can you document that this is your only alternative, and also document, using actual cases, what happens to those who deviate from this policy?)

25

The way the things that I teach relate to the purpose of the school system in which I teach . . .

26

The way the things that I teach relate to the needs of my students . . .

27

The way the things that I teach relate to the community in which I teach . . .

28

Look your partner in the eyes while you respond to this item.
(Also, try to use your partner's name occasionally when responding.)

Right now I'm feeling . . .

29

Read through first.

As a teacher, I believe that I am (very) (reasonably) (not very) successful.

30

Some evidence of my success (or lack of success) includes . . .

31

The methods that I am unhappy using are . . .

32

Methods that I would like to learn more about are . . .

33

My colleagues . . .

34

Checkup: Have a two- or three-minute discussion about this experience so far. Maintain eye contact as much as you can and try to cover the following points:

    a. How well are you listening?
    b. How open and honest have you been?
    c. How eager are you to continue this interchange?
    d. Do you believe that you are getting to know each other?

35

Some educational ideas that I would like to know more about are . . .

36

Ways in which I could improve myself to become a better teacher are . . .

37

Some of my real strengths as a teacher are . . .

38

Some of my real weaknesses as a teacher are . . .

39

Things about myself that I would like to learn more about are . . .

40

If I could begin college all over again I would major in . . .

41

I get feedback from my students about the effectiveness of my teaching by . . .

42

Ideas that I have about teaching that I would like to share with others include . . .

43

A teacher is highly effective when . . .

44

My philosophy of education is . . .

Listening check: "What I hear you saying is . . ."

45

I am (fulfilled) (frustrated) in my teaching because . . .

46

To become a more effective teacher I have to work on (name those that apply):
  a. philosophy
  b. skills such as . . .
  c. subject-matter competency
  d. evaluation (self & others)
  e. other things such as . . .

47

Ideas of yours that have really interested me are . . .

48

Right now the experience is making me feel . . .

49

What I think you need to know is . . .

50

I get the feeling that you . . .

51

Time permitting, you might wish to continue this encounter using topics of your own choosing. You may also deal further with topics mentioned earlier or consider other topics, such as behavior modification, human relations training, teacher organizations, open schools, discipline, education in the future, and the two of you.

13

My Most Unforgettable Teacher: Identifying Effective Traits

Kent D. Beeler

Goals

I. To encourage the participants to reflect on and to describe their most unforgettable teacher.

II. To indicate that the descriptions of unforgettable teachers are highly consistent within a group.

III. To identify traits that teachers and prospective teachers need to develop to become effective teachers.

Group Size

Any number of participants.

Time Required

Forty to fifty minutes is needed for a group of twenty-five participants. The homework task should be assigned to the group one class period prior to its intended use.

Physical Setting

An informal setting or a classroom.

Materials

I. Chalkboard and chalk or newsprint and a felt-tipped marker.

II. Pencils.

Step-by-Step Process

I. The participants are assigned the task of preparing one-page papers describing their most unforgettable teacher. An unusual incident or episode may help describe the teacher.

II. At the following class session, the facilitator asks the participants to exchange themes. As each person reads the other person's paper, he circles words and phrases that describe the unforgettable teacher.

III. The facilitator lists on chalkboard the positive and negative traits and characteristics generated from the themes.

IV. At this point, the facilitator gives a brief review of several studies and research papers (Combs et al., 1974; Witty, 1947) that describe the behaviors and characteristics of effective teachers. These studies may be compared with the descriptions noted in the themes.

V. The facilitator asks the participants to think about the personal characteristics that they consider their strengths. For example, which characteristics are most like the unforgettable teachers and those quoted in the research studies? Which characteristics do the participants need to develop in order to become more effective teachers and people?

VI. The facilitator focuses the discussion on goals for behavioral change.

Variations

I. This activity can be adapted to many groups that want to identify consistent descriptions of unforgettable and effective leaders, supervisors, educators, politicians, etc.

II. Although the one-page papers usually emphasize people with very positive and helpful characteristics, the facilitator may ask some members of the group to write about the worst teacher that they have known.

III. Instead of writing a theme, the participants can be asked to close their eyes and to recall their most unforgettable teacher. They can note the favorable descriptions for class discussion and comparison with research studies.

IV. The focus may take on a different dimension, such as on unforgettable books, trips, competitions, plays, relationships.

References

Combs, A. W., Blume, R. A., Newman, A. J., and Wass, H. L. The professional education of teachers: A humanistic approach to teacher preparation (2nd ed.). Boston: Allyn & Bacon, 1974.

Witty, P. A. The teacher who has helped me most. Elementary English, October 1947, 24, 345-354.

14

Want Ads:
Describing Teacher Styles

Kent D. Beeler

Goals

    I. To encourage teacher trainees to assess their own job potential and marketability in terms of their personal and professional strengths and limitations.

    II. To enable teacher trainees to exchange and to share impressions about themselves.

Group Size

    Any number of participants.

Time Required

    Approximately fifty minutes. Allow five minutes for each participant to share his want ad in the subgroups. The writing activity should be assigned to participants one class period prior to its intended use.

Physical Setting

    Any informal setting.

Materials

    Masking tape or a bulletin board and pins (optional).

Step-by-Step Process

    I. The teacher trainees are asked to prepare a professional-personal teacher want ad for the next class session. The want ad is limited to fifty words and it should focus on the qualities and interests that the teacher trainees value as important in their teaching style and in their lifestyle. The participants may also refer to other items and restrictions related to the type of community, size of school district, subject-grade desired, etc.

The following assumptions are to be made:

1. The trainees are seeking full-time teaching positions in their major fields of study.
2. The want ads will be placed in a newspaper that is circulated in the locale in which they wish to teach.

II. At the following class session, the facilitator divides the participants into small groups to discuss the want ads. Each group selects the most persuasive want ads and notes the reasons for the selections. Discussion also centers on how the trainees felt when developing their want ads.

III. The facilitator reassembles the subgroups into one large group to review the most persuasive want ads. Discussion may follow on how to present one's strengths and teaching qualities to prospective employers and also on how to generalize this practice to obtain employment in a field other than teaching.

IV. The facilitator asks the trainees to circulate their want ads within the large group and then to post them for the group's perusal.

Variations

I. The facilitator may wish to follow this activity with interview training, such as the kind that will be encountered in seeking a teaching position.

II. To add a more realistic dimension, the teacher want ads can be submitted to local school officials or college placement officers who are in charge of hiring or placing professional staff. These persons can be asked to indicate which want ads would prompt them to call the writers for an interview if they were applying for a teaching position.

III. This activity can also be used with people who are entering or reentering the job market on a full- or part-time basis, such as junior or senior high school students, recent retirees, military veterans, housewives, etc. The activity can likewise be used with a group of individuals who are presently employed but who wish to change their place of employment.

IV. Most career education classes at all age levels could use this activity to help students review their strengths and limitations regarding various jobs.

15

My Teaching Field: A Supportive Statement

Kent D. Beeler

Goal

To provide an opportunity for the prospective teacher or the classroom teacher to clarify the immediate and future value of studying a specific teaching field.

Group Size

Any number of participants.

Time Required

Each individual presentation takes approximately ten minutes. An additional five to ten minutes per individual is desirable to permit the audience to respond to his presentation.

Physical Setting

A classroom large enough to accommodate the participants.

Materials

Presenters are expected to bring their own materials, except for chalkboard and chalk. Additional materials may include charts, graphs, audiotapes, slide projectors, screens, and other media equipment.

Step-by-Step Process

I. The facilitator assigns each individual the task of preparing a presentation in support of a specific teaching field. The presentation should be no longer than ten minutes; any audio-visual materials may be used.

II. At the designated class session, each participant gives his presentation to the group. The presenter may ask the audience to assume the role of another group, such as students, curriculum supervisors, or school-board members.

III. Each presenter answers extemporaneously any questions from the audience.

IV. After the question-and-answer session, the facilitator and the observers offer constructive feedback about the content of the presentation, the manner in which it was presented, and the questions and answers raised.

Variations

I. Because class time is usually limited, the facilitator may assign the task to dyads, triads, or small groups for presentation to the class.

II. The facilitator may also work out an arrangement with the university TV productions studio to videotape the sessions and/or the presentations.

III. The facilitator may ask teacher trainees to give their presentations "live" to a group of students whom they might teach.

IV. The format of this experience can be adapted to any situation in which an individual has been asked to justify the continuation of his position or job in terms of his overall contribution to the organization.

V. If class time is not available for presentations, an outline can be prepared by the participants and handed in to the facilitator. It is recommended that each participant incorporate a minimum of five references, three of which can come from classroom teachers, methods class instructors, and students majoring in the same subject-matter field. Over a period of several semesters, the facilitator can compile a lengthy bibliography for use by other students.

16

Helping Professions Inventory: Projecting Potential Conflicts

Kent D. Beeler

Goals

I. To explore the participants' level of acceptance in relating to groups of people who are different politically, religiously, physically/mentally, ethnically/racially, and socially.

II. To project the participants' ability to work professionally with people from a variety of backgrounds.

Group Size

Any number of participants.

Time Required

Approximately fifty minutes for a group of twenty-five.

Physical Setting

Any classroom or informal setting.

Materials

I. A copy of the Helping Professions Inventory for each participant.

II. A copy of the Helping Professions Inventory Scoring Guide for each person.

III. Pencils.

Step-by-Step Process

I. The facilitator explains the purpose of the activity and distributes pencils and copies of the Helping Professions Inventory to the participants.

II. He allows about ten minutes for completion of the inventory.

61

III. When the inventory has been completed, the facilitator circulates copies of the Helping Professions Inventory Scoring Guide and allows approximately ten minutes for the participants to tally their scores.

IV. The facilitator conducts a general discussion and feedback session, based largely on the results of the participants' individual scoring sheets.

 1. The participants are encouraged to share voluntarily at least one response pattern for one of the inventory categories that they recorded on the scoring guide.

 2. Time is allowed for feedback on how the participants felt about completing the inventory, insights gained, confirmations made, questions raised, etc.

 3. The participants examine how they can help overcome the prejudices and barriers reflected in individual responses to the inventory.

V. As a final segment of the discussion, the participants nominate individuals/categories that they would like to add to the Helping Professions Inventory.

Variations

I. Although the inventory is designed primarily for current and future helping persons, it can be used with other populations, especially with groups corresponding to the five categories on the sheet.

II. A brief group discussion may be added between steps II and III to develop a fourth question to be checked on the inventory.

III. The facilitator may add his own fourth question to the inventory. The question may relate to the helping process or could be converted to one of a social nature, such as, "Would you invite this person to a cocktail party at your house?" or "Would you stop and pick up this person if he were hitchhiking on the highway?"

IV. The facilitator may wish to prepare a group response profile of the inventories, which could be accomplished anonymously. Or he could draw the profile on the chalkboard while the group is in session.

V. The inventory may be used in a pre- and post-self-assessment process for prospective helping persons who are in a training workshop on relating to various groups/difficulties.

HELPING PROFESSIONS INVENTORY
Kent D. Beeler

Use the following list of individuals to answer the questions that appear below. Be sure to respond to each question honestly. Do not project your responses in accordance with how you *think* you should answer.

Directions: A. Take one question at a time and follow it through the complete list of individuals in the left column.

B. Place a check mark (✔) in the proper column for each individual to whom you would answer "No." Also place a check mark if you have to hesitate before answering "Yes."

Question No. 1: Do I feel I can greet this person warmly and welcome him sincerely?

Question No. 2: Do I feel I can accept him honestly as he is and be comfortable enough to listen to his problems?

Question No. 3: Do I feel I can say genuinely that I would try to help him come to grips with his problems as they relate to or arise from the label-stereotype given him here?

Question No. 4: _____

Individuals	Question No. 1	Question No. 2	Question No. 3	Question No. 4
1. Oriental-American				
2. Unmarried Expectant Mother				
3. Jew				
4. Amputee				
5. Neo-Nazi				
6. Mexican-American				
7. Family Deserter				
8. Catholic				
9. Senile Senior Citizen				
10. John Bircher				

Individuals	Question No. 1	Question No. 2	Question No. 3	Question No. 4
11. American Indian				
12. Prostitute				
13. Christian Scientist				
14. Cerebral Palsied Person				
15. Black Panther				
16. Italian-American				
17. Homosexual				
18. Atheist				
19. Blind Person				
20. Communist				
21. Black American				
22. Drug Pusher				
23. Jehovah's Witness				
24. Mental Retardate				
25. Ku Klux Klansman				
26. White Anglo-Saxon American				
27. Alcoholic				
28. Mormon				
29. Person with a Facial Disfiguration				
30. Student for a Democratic Society				

HELPING PROFESSIONS INVENTORY SCORING GUIDE

This guide has been prepared to see if you projected some difficulty in working with specific clienteles listed on the Helping Professions Inventory.

The thirty types of individuals listed on the inventory can be grouped into five categories: ethnic/racial, social problems, religious, physically/mentally handicapped, and political. You are to transfer your check marks from the Helping Professions Inventory to this form.

If you notice a concentration of checks (a) within a specific category of individuals or (b) under any specific question, this may indicate a conflict that could hinder you from rendering professional help.

Categories	Question No. 1	Question No. 2	Question No. 3	Question No. 4
Ethnic/Racial				
1. Oriental-American				
6. Mexican-American				
11. American Indian				
16. Italian-American				
21. Black American				
26. White Anglo-Saxon American				
Social Problems				
2. Unmarried Expectant Mother				
7. Family Deserter				
12. Prostitute				
17. Homosexual				
22. Drug Pusher				
27. Alcoholic				

Categories	Question No. 1	Question No. 2	Question No. 3	Question No. 4
Religious				
3. Jew				
8. Catholic				
13. Christian Scientist				
18. Atheist				
23. Jehovah's Witness				
28. Mormon				
Physically/Mentally Handicapped				
4. Amputee				
9. Senile Senior Citizen				
14. Cerebral Palsied Person				
19. Blind Person				
24. Mental Retardate				
29. Person with a Facial Disfiguration				
Political				
5. Neo-Nazi				
10. John Bircher				
15. Black Panther				
20. Communist				
25. Ku Klux Klansman				
30. Student for a Democratic Society				

17

Station-Seeking Radio:
A Fantasy on Educational Experiences*

Frederick H. McCarty, Bernard Nisenholz, and Russell Kraus

Goals

   I. To help the participants identify those educational practices that they would like to utilize with their own learning groups.

  II. To discover similarities and differences in the participants' educational experiences.

Group Size

A class that can be divided into small groups of four to six people.

Time Required

Approximately forty minutes.

Physical Setting

Preferably an informal setting with comfortable seating.

Step-by-Step Process

   I. The facilitator asks the participants to experience a fantasy designed to help them identify educational experiences that they would like to utilize or learn from. For approximately ten minutes, he guides them through the following fantasy. (After each stimulus statement in the fantasy, the facilitator pauses for approximately thirty seconds.)

  II. (Relaxation.) The facilitator asks the participants to become comfortable, take several deep breaths, close their eyes, and relax.

---

*From "Awareness Experiences for Elementary School Teachers," by F. H. McCarty, B. Nisenholz, & R. Kraus, *Journal of Teacher Education*, 1972, 23(4), 457-460. Copyright © 1972 by American Association of Colleges for Teacher Education, 1201 Sixteenth Street, N.W., Washington, D.C. 20036. Adapted and reprinted by permission.

III. (Fantasy.) The facilitator says, "We are going on a short fantasy trip. I will be your guide. Imagine that your mind is a radio with nine stations. The stations symbolize your kindergarten year and grades one through eight. Let your tuning dial roam up and down the stations. [The facilitator pauses to provide time for the participants to fantasize roaming up and down the imaginary radio dial.] Focus for a few seconds on the experiences you see as you pass each station. [Pause] Now, tune in to one really loud and clear station. What is the program about? Is it happy? Sad? Friendly? Terrifying? What details come to mind? What people are participating? What is the content of the program? What do you like especially? What do you wish to change in the program? For a few seconds, hold the focus on this station so that you can remember the events, your feelings and thoughts, and the things that you valued then. Slowly, I would like you to stretch your arms and legs. Open your eyes and look around. Is everyone okay?"

IV. The facilitator divides the group into small groups of four to six people and asks the participants to share their experiences and feelings about the fantasy. Each group chooses a spokesman to report back to the large group. (Twenty minutes.)

V. The large group reassembles and the spokesmen report on the experiences that were related in their groups.

VI. The facilitator initiates a discussion emphasizing the following points:
1. Were there noticeable similarities and differences in the experiences?
2. What was the ratio of positive to negative experiences and feelings?
3. Were attitudes and behaviors toward school and learning formed during those years?

VII. The facilitator focuses the discussion on the part of the fantasy that could be used to establish a better teaching-learning classroom experience. The participants are asked to formulate and share one goal for action.

Variations

I. The fantasy may be rewritten to focus on selected or different grade levels.

II. The stimulus statements can be changed to recall people and/or relationships.

III. The short fantasy can focus on any number of other topics, such as family relationships, community activities, religious festivities, or recreational trips.

IV. Other groups can use the fantasy to reveal the development of attitudes and beliefs about education.

18

The Magic Wand:
Developing a Humanistic Curriculum

Frederick H. McCarty

Goals

 I. To increase the participants' awareness of the relationship between their own motivations about teaching and the need for a humanistic emphasis in curriculum.

 II. To free the participants temporarily from the restraints normally imposed upon their "curricular imagination" by their own fantasies of what is acceptable in school settings.

Group Size

Ten to thirty people. The participants interact in small groups of six to eight people.

Time Required

One and one-half hours.

Physical Setting

A room large enough for each group to be seated comfortably in a circle, well separated from the other groups.

Materials

Paper and pencils.

Step-by-Step Process

 I. The facilitator asks the participants to find a comfortable place in the room and to relax by breathing deeply and stretching their muscles.

 II. After a bit of relaxing, he tells them that he is about to guide them through a fantasy that will be effective only to the extent that they allow themselves to participate.

III. The facilitator asks the participants to close their eyes. (He may lower the room lighting somewhat.) As he begins the fantasy, he speaks slowly and softly, pausing for a few seconds at appropriate places.

IV. (Fantasy.) The facilitator says, "You have a magic wand. With it you can eliminate any restraints you may feel about what it is possible to do in school. Imagine that you are in a school building. It is a new building with many comfortable, carpeted rooms and plenty of resources, such as books and films, computer terminals, games, toys, tools, and various kinds of equipment. [Pause] The children come into your room. They sit around you on cushions on the floor. [Pause] You know that you are really free to do anything that you think is healthy with these kids. [Pause] If you need anything, a wave of your magic wand will get it; if there is an obstacle, the wand will remove it. The school board is on your side. [Pause] If anyone complains, a wave of your wand will help them to become more understanding. [Pause] There are no curricula, requirements, tests, or grades. [Pause] For the next few minutes, imagine what you would want to *do* with these kids [Pause]; what you would want to have them learn [Pause]; what you would want them to *know* [Pause]; how you would want them to *feel* [Pause]; how you would involve them in planning their learning experiences [Pause]; how you would involve parents in the school planning and experiences [Pause]; how you would describe your relationship with the learners, parents, administrators, the community." [Pause] After two to four minutes of *complete* silence, the facilitator asks the participants to open their eyes.

V. The facilitator divides the group into small groups of six to eight people. Each group is asked to sit in a small, closed circle, well separated from the other groups. No tables, chairs, or other obstacles should obstruct the people in each group. The participants are asked to share their "fantasy curricula" with each other. Throughout this process, the facilitator travels quietly from group to group, helping to keep the focus on the task. He especially watches for people who block the process by saying "Yes, but . . .," e.g., "Yes, but in the real world they won't let you do that."

VI. After considering the fantasy curricula, the participants focus on the constraints that the real world imposes, e.g., established curricula, budgets, differing educational philosophies, disapproval by other colleagues or administrators, parental disapproval. (No more than ten minutes.)

VII. Then the facilitator says, "OK, here's the challenge. Considering all the pressures that you have discussed, spend some real energy right now discussing how much of your fantasy curricula you can introduce into your learning group: All of it? Some of it? Which parts? Be somewhat practical and specific. Try to imagine fitting one part of it into the activities of a real classroom. How would you handle some of those potential problems and pressures?"

VIII. The facilitator encourages each person to establish at least one goal to work on during the coming week. He distributes pencils and paper, and asks the participants to write down the goal and some specific aspects of it. At the next group session, they will share their accomplishments.

Variations

I. The content and focus of the fantasy trip can be adapted to other settings in which new approaches are sought.

II. Classroom students in elementary school or high school may be involved in planning the learning approach for the classroom by using the fantasy trip.

III. The facilitator may give assignments on developing action modes after step VII.

IV. The structured experience can easily be used with various groups that are interested in and/or working for school/curricula changes. It can be used as a brainstorming, problem-solving process for various school problems by slightly adjusting the focus to fit a different situation.

References

Thatcher, D. *Teaching, loving, and self-directed learning.* Pacific Palisades, Calif.: Goodyear, 1973.

Weinstein, G., & Fantini, M. D. *Toward humanistic education: A curriculum of affect.* New York: Praeger, 1970.

19

Teaching-Learning Goals:
Steps Toward Achievement

Frederick H. McCarty

Goals

I. To encourage the participants to identify their professional strengths and weaknesses.

II. To help the participants identify steps toward achieving their goals.

III. To emphasize the need for a commitment to achievement on the part of the participants.

Group Size

Small groups of four to six members each.

Time Required

A minimum of one and one-half hours to a maximum of two hours.

Physical Setting

Any comfortable, quiet room in which each group's chairs can be arranged in a circle.

Materials

Paper, pencils (or pens), and envelopes.

Step-by-Step Process

I. The facilitator asks the participants to form groups of four to six people. Each group arranges its chairs in a circle.

II. The facilitator distributes two sheets of paper, a pencil, and an envelope to each participant. He asks the participants to list five professional strengths that they possess that will be useful in their teaching careers. These strengths may consist of skills, areas of knowledge, traits, values, etc.

III. The facilitator encourages each participant to share with his group as many of the strengths on his list as he feels comfortable in sharing. (Two minutes per participant.)

IV. The facilitator asks the participants to write another list consisting of five professional weaknesses—deficiencies that are *possible to correct,* such as courses not yet taken, books yet unread, activities that are crucial but have not been experienced, or skills seen as desirable but not yet mastered.

V. The participants relate items that they wish to share from their lists of weaknesses.

VI. The facilitator emphasizes the importance of establishing goals. He asks all participants to list five *steps* toward achieving their professional goals. He defines professional goals as a combination of (a) remediation of deficiencies and (b) polishing and refining old skills and qualities. Participants may wish to focus only on one or two of their more important professional goals. In addition, they list several "*drags*"—forces that tend to keep them from achieving their goals.

VII. Focusing on one person at a time, each group listens to the participants' lists of *steps* and *drags,* makes suggestions of steps that they have not noted, asks which of the steps they can work on *right now,* and, finally, notes one of their earlier mentioned strengths on which they can capitalize.

VIII. As a final step, the facilitator asks each person to write a short note to himself, which may start with one of the following sentence stems:
   1. "I'm going to start to work right away on a selected professional goal by. . . ."
   2. "By ___(date)___ I will have started to change and grow in the direction of my professional goal because I will already have . . . ."
   3. "During the next five days, I am going to capitalize on one strength of mine by . . . ."

The participants seal the notes in the envelopes. They may take them home or, if some participants wish, the envelopes can be addressed and mailed. Participants may wish to exchange the letters and agree to mail them at some later, agreed-upon date to serve as an additional boost to motivation.

Variations

I. This activity can be focused on any chosen field. Personal goals may be emphasized rather than career goals.

II. The activity may also be useful in career education classes for students to set goals for the future.

III. In step VII, each person may have a card on which other group members can write down *positive* comments and ideas for the person to take with him.

IV. Contracts may be prepared between the facilitator and the participants to motivate them to reach some of their goals.

20

Two Teaching Styles: An Experience in Affecting Classroom Climate

Gary F. Render and Paula K. Horvatich

Goal

To assess the potential effects of a teacher's manner, attitudes, and personality on the classroom climate.

Group Size

Any size group of teacher trainees.

Time Required

Approximately one hour.

Physical Setting

A comfortable room.

Materials

Several sheets of unlined white paper and several crayons of various colors for each participant.

Step-by-Step Process

I. The facilitator explains that the class will be involved in a role play in which he will assume several roles and the participants will just be themselves.

II. The facilitator distributes the paper and crayons and tells the participants to do whatever they want to do with the material. He may offer some suggestions, e.g., poetry, drawings, plans for bulletin boards.

III. The facilitator circulates throughout the class and praises the students' work. He is generally supportive and encourages the students to share their materials, ideas, and products.

IV. He tells the participants that he must leave the room for a few minutes, during which time they should continue without him.

V. After standing outside of the room for a few minutes, the facilitator reenters the classroom and introduces himself as "Mr. Jones." He tells the class that he will be in charge until the other instructor returns. "Mr. Jones" informs the students to continue with what they were doing so that he can evaluate their work.

VI. "Mr. Jones" suddenly announces that the students' work is generally unproductive. He instructs them to put away everything except one sheet of paper and one crayon.

VII. The instructor gives many directions and chastises the students for not following his instructions. "Mr. Jones" also ridicules them and destroys their work. He appears to the students as an authoritative and hostile figure.

VIII. The instructor maintains this role until the students are convinced that he is really "Mr. Jones" and they become sullen, withdrawn, subservient, and somewhat critical of each other.

IX. The instructor then announces that he must leave the room and that they should sit straight in their seats with their hands folded and remain silent until the other instructor returns.

X. After waiting outside of the room for a few minutes, the facilitator returns and informs the group that he will no longer assume a role. He asks the participants to discuss their reactions and impressions during various parts of the activity.

XI. The facilitator continues the discussion to expand the participants' awareness of the impact of the instructor's affective behavior. Emphasis should be placed on how they felt about working under both conditions.

XII. The facilitator asks the group to develop a simple check list that would help teachers review the affective aspects of their behavior and how it affects the learning climate. Participants are asked to supply the rationale for each item on the check list and to rely heavily on their own learning experiences.

Variations

I. Step XII may be assigned as homework rather than used as part of the discussion.

II. The facilitator may ask a colleague who is not known to the group to play the role of "Mr. Jones" and then to participate in the discussion.

III. The facilitator may play the role of "Mr. Jones" first and then change his role to that of a supporting, encouraging instructor.

IV. An adapted version of this activity may be used to demonstrate different types of small-group leadership behavior. A discussion topic may be substituted for the paper and crayons assignment.

V. The facilitator may wish to "stack the deck" by secretly involving one or two students in the role-play situations. For example, these students might react very negatively to "Mr. Jones" and try to coerce the group into leaving.

21

Teaching Concerns Focus Game: Exploring Solutions

Bernard Nisenholz and Frederick H. McCarty

Goals

I. To increase the participants' awareness of their present concerns about being or becoming teachers.

II. To explore alternative responses to these teacher-related concerns.

Group Size

A class of ten to thirty people that can be divided into subgroups of approximately four each.

Time Required

Two hours.

Physical Setting

A classroom or an informal lounge area.

Materials

I. Paper and pencils.

II. Two wheel diagrams for each participant. The outer circle should be four inches in diameter. The inner circle should be one inch in diameter.

Wheel Diagram

III. A copy of the Rules for Focus for each participant.

Step-by-Step Process

I. The facilitator distributes the paper, pencils, and two wheel diagrams to each participant and explains the nature of the activity.

II. He tells the participants to write the word "concerns" in the inner circle of the first wheel. He asks them to close their eyes and imagine their concerns about becoming teachers. The participants list the concerns in the spokes of the first wheel until they have identified and filled in four concerns.

III. Each participant is instructed to concentrate on the concerns until one in particular seems to stand out as most important. The participants write that concern in the inner circle of the second wheel.

IV. The facilitator asks the participants to "get in touch" with their feelings when they think about that one concern.

V. The participants list those feelings on the four spokes of the second wheel. A completed pair of wheels might look like this:

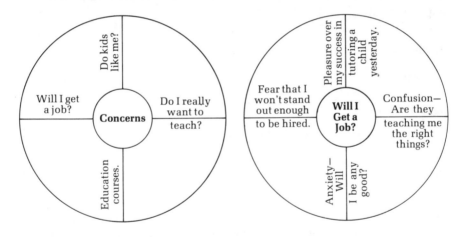

VI. The facilitator divides the participants into small groups of four each.

VII. He provides each participant with a copy of the Rules for Focus for group discussion. (Five minutes to read.)

VIII. The facilitator indicates that the participants have approximately one hour to share and focus on each other's concerns. During this period, the facilitator moves from group to group to help focus on the concerns and the solutions.

IX. After each participant has had an opportunity to be the focus person, the activity is completed. There is no need for a large group debriefing. Some final processing may be done in the small groups, using the following questions: Did you feel that you were listened to and helped in dealing with your concern? How closely were the Rules for Focus followed? Give positive feedback to someone in the group who helped you by describing specific behaviors. For example, "When you pointed out how I contradicted myself, I was able to sort out my confusion."

Variations

I. Observers may be selected in each group to provide feedback on the interactive group process, e.g., helping and hindering aspects, roles played, norms established.

II. A second concern from the first wheel may be considered at the next session or may be used for a written assignment.

III. The concerns may be discussed in dyads or triads with more persons serving in a helping role. More than the four original concerns may be covered.

IV. The process may be used by groups other than prospective teachers, such as paraprofessionals, school helpers, school boards, parent-teacher organizations, etc. The focus for concerns can be easily adapted to other school programs.

V. The content and format may be adapted to different situations for individuals and groups who are attempting to focus on primary concerns and reach alternative solutions.

RULES FOR FOCUS

1. In the basic focus game, any group member may keep the focus for any topic for as long as he wishes unless topic or time limitations are agreed upon in advance.
2. When the focus slips from a group member, either inadvertently or because someone else takes it, the focus should return to whom it belonged. The first few times the group plays the game, it is helpful if the focus person designates a monitor to enforce the rules, thus freeing the focus person from having to defend his own rights.
3. When the focus person is finished, he should announce that he is relinquishing the focus. *He should not let it gradually slip away.*
4. Retain the topic originally raised by the focus. If the discussion drifts, a group member or the monitor should refocus the topic.
5. Honesty is important; overstatements should be avoided. The effectiveness of the game is seriously impaired when group members cannot trust each other's communications.
6. Each group member has responsibility for enhancing the group climate. Each person should take the initiative within the limits of the rules to help the other members feel secure, appreciated, and understood.
7. *No official leader is required* for the game and no privileges or penalties are permitted for any group leader who happens to be present.

22

Labeling Students: Potential Dangers

Louis Thayer

Goal

To help teacher and counselor trainees become sensitive to the hazards of labeling students and predicting student potential without thorough and careful study.

Group Size

Twenty to thirty teacher or counselor trainees or people involved in human relations training.

Time Required

One hour. The descriptive statement should be assigned to the participants one class period (or up to one week) prior to its intended use.

Physical Setting

A classroom in which the group regularly meets.

Materials

A copy of the Labeling Students Case Sheet for each student.

Step-by-Step Process

I. The facilitator asks the students to write a short anecdotal report based on their observations of a child under the age of sixteen. The statement, limited to sixty words or less, should consist of descriptive phrases and adjectives. Only a fictitious name should be mentioned in the description. The facilitator offers several examples of behavioral descriptions that might be used in the anecdotal statements. He asks the students to prepare the assignment for the next class meeting.

II. Before the class is dismissed, the facilitator asks four to six people to stay after class. He asks these students to write the assignment based on their own childhood and in terms of how significant others may have perceived them before the age of sixteen. The facilitator cautions these students *not* to reveal their assignment to the other students.

III. At the designated class period, the facilitator divides the students into small groups of six to eight persons to discuss their anecdotal statements.

IV. He collects the papers from each group and distributes them to another group.

V. Each person reads the paper he receives to the others in his group. Then the other group members try to predict each child's future development. For example, in five years, will each child be designated as gifted, average/normal, psychotic, neurotic, delinquent, or mentally deficient? The facilitator encourages the students to discuss the cases and to keep individual records of their predictions. One person in each group may keep a tally of the group consensus on each child.

VI. After the groups complete their discussions and predictions, the facilitator distributes copies of the Labeling Students Case Sheet. Each group discusses each case and reaches group consensus on predicting the child's future development.

VII. Each group shares with the total class some of the comments that were made as the group predicted each child's future development.

VIII. The facilitator reads the names of the people who were described on the case sheet:
Case 1: Eleanor Roosevelt
Case 2: Albert Einstein
Case 3: Thomas Edison.
He emphasizes how hasty judgments based on incomplete evidence can affect people's lives.

IX. The facilitator reveals that a number of the anecdotal statements reviewed earlier were written about actual members of the class. He may ask the students to attempt to identify the classmates who were described.

X. The facilitator asks each person who wrote about himself to read his anecdotal report and to discuss briefly some of the perceptions held by significant others in his life. Discussion can continue according to level of interest and time limitations.

Variations

I. If time is limited, the facilitator may omit the assignment and base the discussions and predictions solely on the case sheet.

II. The students may be told in step III that some of the statements describe actual members of the class.

Reference

Goertzel, V., & Goertzel, M. G. *Cradles of eminence.* Boston: Little, Brown & Co., 1962, pp. xii-xiii.

LABELING STUDENTS CASE SHEET

In five years, will each of the following children be designated as gifted, average/normal, psychotic, neurotic, delinquent, or mentally deficient?

Case 1

Girl, age sixteen, orphaned, willed to custody of grandmother by mother, who was separated from alcoholic husband, now deceased. Mother rejected the homely child, who has been proven to lie and to steal sweets. Swallowed penny to attract attention at five. Father was fond of child. Child lived in fantasy as the mistress of father's household for years. Four young uncles and aunts in household cannot be managed by the grandmother, who is widowed. Young uncle drinks; has left home without telling the grandmother his destination. Aunt, emotional over love affair, locks self in room. Grandmother resolves to be more strict with granddaughter since she fears she has failed with own children. Dresses granddaughter oddly. Refused to let her have playmates, put her in braces to keep back straight. Did not send her to grade school. Aunt on paternal side of family crippled; uncle asthmatic.

Case 2

Boy, senior year secondary school, has obtained certificate from physician stating that nervous breakdown makes it necessary for him to leave school for six months. Boy not a good all-around student; has no friends —teachers find him a problem—spoke late—father ashamed of son's lack of athletic ability—poor adjustment to school. Boy has odd mannerisms, makes up own religion, chants hymns to himself—parents regard him as "different."

Case 3

Boy, age six; head large at birth. Thought to have had brain fever. Three siblings died before his birth. Mother does not agree with relatives and neighbors that child is probably abnormal. Child sent to school—diagnosed as mentally ill by teacher. Mother is angry—withdraws child from school, says she will teach him herself.

These cases are taken from V. Goertzel & M. G. Goertzel, *Cradles of Eminence,* Boston: Little, Brown & Co., 1962, pp. xii-xiii. Reprinted by permission.

23

Thinking Out Loud: Building Communication Skills

Vincent Peterson

Goals

I. To provide practice in using interpersonal communication skills: probing, empathic listening, building upon ideas, synthesizing, and receiving feedback in a group setting.

II. To help the participants focus on the ideas of others rather than on their own (to become more *thou* centered than *I* centered).

III. To involve the participants in a content area.

IV. To heighten awareness of the effects of group processes in thinking about and generating ideas.

Group Size

Any number of groups of six participants each. Although the activity is designed for junior high school students or adults, it can be adapted for younger groups.

Time Required

Approximately one and one-half hours.

Physical Setting

One or more rooms large enough for the groups to interact without disturbing each other.

Materials

I. A copy of the Thinking Out Loud Group Member Directions Sheet for each participant.

II. A copy of the Thinking Out Loud Discussion Topics Sheet for each participant.

III. A copy of the Thinking Out Loud Observer-Judge Guidelines Sheet for each observer-judge.

IV. A copy of the Thinking Out Loud Participant Self-Evaluation Form for each group member.

V. Pencils.

Step-by-Step Process

I. The facilitator gives a brief review (or lecturette) on the skills of open and closed probing, empathic listening, building upon ideas, and synthesizing in interpersonal communication.

II. He then divides the participants into groups of six people and selects one member in each group to act as an observer-judge.

III. The facilitator distributes the Thinking Out Loud Group Member Directions Sheets and the Thinking Out Loud Discussion Topics Sheets. He distributes a Thinking Out Loud Observer-Judge Guidelines Sheet, five Thinking Out Loud Participant Self-Evaluation Forms, and six pencils to each observer-judge.

IV. The facilitator briefly describes the group members' directions and defines the role of the observer-judge. The groups are told that an observer-judge will interrupt the activity if a participant deviates from the directions. After answering any remaining questions, the facilitator tells the groups to begin the discussion.

V. At the conclusion of the thirty-minute time period, the facilitator stops the discussions. The observer-judges distribute pencils and the Thinking Out Loud Participant Self-Evaluation Forms. (Allow five minutes for group members to complete the forms.)

VI. When the forms are completed, each observer-judge offers feedback to each member of his group. Then each group member discusses how he perceived his participation in the group. The other group members and the observer-judge offer their own feedback.

VII. The total group reconvenes to process the activity. The facilitator should focus on identifying strengths and weaknesses in communicating and the use of these communication skills in other group settings.

Variations

I. A second observer could be used to check out other group process variables, such as actual patterns of interaction between individuals within the group.

II. Using the same basic format, but changing the specific skills, this activity can be used to sharpen skills in conflict resolution, attaining consensus in a group, etc.

III. The activity can be used as a form of pre- and post-test assessment for students in teacher or counselor education courses.

IV. Prior to the actual discussions, one small group can begin the discussion in a fishbowl arrangement in the middle of the room with the facilitator serving as the observer-judge.

V. The facilitator can hold a special training session with the observer-judges prior to the small-group activity.

VI. The Thinking Out Loud Participant Self-Evaluation Forms may be used to focus on self-perceptions compared with "other" perceptions.

THINKING OUT LOUD GROUP MEMBER DIRECTIONS SHEET

I. Do not select a leader for your group.

II. As a group, quickly select a topic for the discussion (one minute). Use the Thinking Out Loud Discussion Topics Sheet or select a topic of your choice.

III. After the topic is selected, use your skills in probing, empathic listening, clarifying, and integrating (synthesizing) to discover what each member of the group thinks about the chosen topic. *Do not state your opinion or elaborate on your point of view unless another person specifically requests it.*

YOUR BASIC TASK IS TO HELP OTHER MEMBERS IN YOUR GROUP EXPRESS THEMSELVES, TO BUILD UPON THEIR IDEAS, AND, WHEREVER POSSIBLE, TO INTEGRATE THEM WITH NEW IDEAS.

IV. Use the following steps to focus on the contributions of others in your group:
1. Use *probing* and *empathic understanding* responses to discover how *other* members of your group think and feel about the topic.
2. Try to add a personal contribution by *building* upon the ideas of others. (This process should be done succinctly.)
3. Try to integrate the ideas of two or more group members (including yourself) into a new or refined idea.
4. Avoid putting down anyone else's point of view. This does not mean, however, that you cannot state a different point of view.
5. Give other group members an opportunity to probe, clarify, etc. If a group member appears to dominate the conversation, try to bring the conversation back to the original focus.

V. When a topic has been exhausted, move on to a new topic. You do not have to attain a consensus of opinion or any other measure of agreement on any of these issues.

THINKING OUT LOUD DISCUSSION TOPICS SHEET

The topics can be designed to fit any content area. These suggested topics focus on working and relating to students.

I. Should a teacher's job include helping students to enjoy school and learning? If so, how can a teacher best accomplish this task?

II. What type of learning environment is best for maximum student learning?

III. How open should a teacher be with his students?
   1. How should a teacher deal with his feelings in the classroom?
   2. How should a teacher deal with the feelings of students in a classroom?
   3. How close (friendly) should a teacher be with his students?

IV. How can a teacher help students to learn to practice thinking in the classroom?

V. Ways to deal with the motivation of students are...

VI. Can a classroom environment be designed so that there are few, if any, discipline problems? If so, how?

VII. What should the teacher's relationship be to the student?
   1. Parent-child.
   2. Adult-adult.
   3. Other.

VIII. What other topic would you like to discuss?

THINKING OUT LOUD OBSERVER-JUDGE GUIDELINES SHEET

Your main task is to record on the Tally Sheet the types of statements made by each member of your group by placing check marks in the column corresponding to the responses made.

You should intervene in the group process *only* if one or more group members monopolize the discussion.

At the conclusion of the discussion, distribute a pencil and a Participant Self-Evaluation Form to each member of your group. After the forms are completed, you should use the data on the Tally Sheet to provide feedback to each group member on his communication pattern. Later the group members can compare their own self-evaluations with your observations.

Tally Sheet

Types of Responses	Member				
	1	2	3	4	5

Probing
    Open-ended
    Closed					

Empathic Understanding
    (How often did he try to be sure he
    knew what the other person was
    saying?)					

Building
    (How often did he add on to the ideas
    of another participant?)					

Synthesizing
    (How often did he try to pull ideas
    together?)					

"I (my)" Statements
    (How often did he offer his own ideas
    or experiences without being asked
    by another?)					

Other observations					
Total number of responses					

Tally of "New Ideas" generated by interaction _____

THINKING OUT LOUD PARTICIPANT SELF-EVALUATION FORM

Name_____

Directions: On the form below estimate the types of responses that you made during the previous group discussion. Use the last column to record the observations of the observer-judge.

	My Estimate	Observer-Judge's Estimate
I. Probing		
Open-ended	_____	_____
Closed	_____	_____
II. Empathic Understanding		
(How often did I try to be sure I knew what the other person was saying?)	_____	_____
III. Building		
(How often did I add on to the ideas of another participant?)	_____	_____
IV. Synthesizing		
(How often did I try to pull ideas together?)	_____	_____
V. "I (my)" Statements		
(How often did I offer my ideas or experiences without being asked by another?)	_____	_____
VI. How many other types of responses did I give?	_____	_____
VII. Total number of responses made during the discussion.	_____	_____
VIII. Number of new ideas generated by group interaction.	_____	_____

Comments on my own group participation: _____

24

Classroom Rules: A Discussion Stimulus

Louis Thayer

Goals

I. To help prospective teachers review their experiences with and present and past attitudes toward classroom rules.

II. To stimulate the formulation of classroom expectations.

Group Size

This activity works well with a class of fifteen to thirty teacher trainees.

Time Required

Approximately twenty minutes. Time requirements vary depending on the amount of time needed for the class to react, verbally or nonverbally, to the rules sheet.

Physical Setting

A classroom.

Materials

A copy of the Classroom Rules Sheet for each member of the class.

Step-by-Step Process

I. The instructor stands near the classroom door at the beginning of the first or second class session, before the students know his classroom expectations, and hands out a copy of the Classroom Rules Sheet to each student arriving for class.

II. Remaining oblivious to the students' reactions, the instructor proceeds with a lesson unrelated to the Classroom Rules Sheet. He does not discuss the rules until there are excessive verbal or nonverbal student reactions or until it becomes obvious that there are many questions concerning the rules.

III. At this point, the instructor encourages the students to share and clarify their reactions to the stimulus statement. He also helps them relate which thoughts, emotions, and perceptions are related to their public school experiences and which are related to their college experiences.

IV. The instructor then initiates a discussion on the relationship between the students' past experiences and the behaviors that they are currently developing on classroom expectations and the formulation of expectations. Often many teachers have preconceived attitudes and values about classroom behavior that date back to their high school and college years.

V. The facilitator divides the large group into several subgroups to brainstorm ways of formulating expectations on student and teacher behavior in the classroom.

VI. The large group reconvenes, and the instructor asks the students to share the ideas generated in the subgroups.

Variations

I. The brainstorm session in step V may focus on very specific topics concerning classroom expectations, such as participation in class activities, talking in class, discussion behavior, student input in classroom rules, and the effects of school policy on teacher and student classroom behavior.

II. The classroom rules stimulus statement can be modified to fit individual situations.

III. The instructor may wish to use the stimulus statement in a "what if" situation, i.e., "What if these were my classroom rules?" Then the discussion could proceed without actually provoking students at the beginning of the class session.

Notes

The idea for this activity came from Herbert Kohl, author of *36 Children,* who used it with audiences to help them remember what they felt like in school classrooms.

Reference

Kohl, H. *36 children.* New York: Signet Books, 1968.

CLASSROOM RULES SHEET

Observe these classroom rules:

1. Do not arrive late for class or leave early without permission.

2. Use alternate seating—male, female, male, etc.

3. No talking when the professor is lecturing.

4. Do not bring food or beverages to class.

5. Everyone will participate in all class activities.

6. Pay attention to all class discussions and take notes.

7. No smoking or chewing gum.

25

Classroom Sketch: Identifying the Primary Focus

Kent D. Beeler

Goals

I. To help students, teachers, and prospective teachers examine their perceptions and impressions of what a classroom primarily represents.

II. To focus on the importance of learners as the primary concern in a classroom.

Group Size

Any number of participants.

Time Required

Approximately fifty to sixty minutes for a group of twenty participants. Each sketch with accompanying commentary entails about two or three minutes per participant.

Materials

I. A pencil and two sheets of white, unlined 8½″ x 11″ paper for each person.

II. An opaque projector or masking tape (optional).

Step-by-Step Process

I. The facilitator distributes the pencils and paper to the participants and asks them to sketch a classroom. The participants are told to use simplistic designs for their sketches. (Ten to fifteen minutes.)

II. When the participants have completed their sketches, the facilitator asks them to write a brief description of their classrooms on the other sheet of paper.

III. If an opaque projector is used, the facilitator collects the sketches and descriptions and displays the sketches one at a time. Alternatively, the sketches may be posted on the wall.

IV. The facilitator encourages the participants to describe what they see in each sketch and what appears to be missing. Then he reads the brief description attached to the sketch and asks the writer for any additional comments. Sketches often focus on furniture and furnishings (chairs, tables, chalkboards, etc.) and neglect the individuals and their life-space needs within a learning setting.

V. As the showing and discussion process continues, the facilitator lists various aspects of focus in the sketches that point toward or away from the learner as the central focus of the classroom experience.

Variations

I. This same type of activity can be related to the objects or persons in the physical environment of other organizations, institutions, agencies, etc.

II. If the facilitator desires the participants to draw a more elaborate sketch, the task may be assigned as homework for the next group session.

26

Random Rules and Capricious Consequences: Using Power Effectively

Francis M. Aversano and Robert L. Bodine

Goals

I. To demonstrate how the arbitrary misuse of power by the leader or teacher can frustrate, annoy, or simply "turn off" participants.

II. To demonstrate the importance of using power wisely and sharing power.

III. To facilitate the expression of frustrations induced by arbitrary reward systems.

Group Size

Any number of small groups of five persons each.

Time Required

Fifty minutes.

Physical Setting

A comfortable setting in which several small groups can work without distracting each other.

Materials

I. A copy of the Random Rules and Capricious Consequences Group Leader's Instructions Sheet for each appointed leader.

II. Paper and pencils.

Step-by-Step Process

I. The facilitator divides the participants into groups of five persons each. He randomly appoints a group leader for each group and distributes the paper and pencils. He hands a copy of the Random Rules and Capricious Consequences Group Leader's Instructions

Sheet to each group leader and allows time for the leaders to read their directions.

II. The group leaders conduct three games with the members of their groups. (Fifteen minutes.)

III. After the scoring is completed, the facilitator asks the participants to form one large group to discuss the games, the rules, and the leaders. He encourages them to relate some of their feelings of frustration and resentment concerning their participation.

IV. The facilitator reviews the rules of the games and directs the discussion toward the use and misuse of power. Other areas may also be discussed:

1. How might situations like games 2 and 3 cause "losers" to stop participating in learning situations?

2. What did games 2 and 3 have to say to you about classroom rules?

3. What were your feelings toward the leader during games 1, 2, and 3?

4. How did it feel to discover and/or not to discover the rule in game 1?

5. How did you all feel about the games after you found out the rules?

6. What were your reactions to having everything you said be wrong in the latter two games?

7. How did your perceptions of the winner and/or leader change in games 2 and 3?

8. How might similar situations with hidden rules be inadvertently created in a learning group discussion (e.g., only special textbook words may be accepted by the facilitator)?

Variations

I. The "rules" may need to be modified to fit more adequately the age level of the participants.

II. Game 3 may be omitted if there is a lack of time.

RANDOM RULES AND CAPRICIOUS CONSEQUENCES
GROUP LEADER'S INSTRUCTIONS SHEET

You will conduct three games with the members of your group. The instructions for each game are the same (see instructions below). Discuss the instructions and the method of scoring with your group.

Reveal the rule of the game only if a group member guesses it. Otherwise, tell the group members that they must wait until the three games are completed. At the completion of the three games, go over the game answers and ask each group member to total his score to see who is the winner.

Instructions: "I will ask you a question and you should answer as quickly as possible. You will receive two points for each correct answer. If you can guess why your answers were acceptable (i.e., guess the rule of the game), you will receive a bonus of twenty points at the end of the game. The person with the most points at the end of five minutes wins. Each person should keep his own score."

Game 1

Q. Name the states in the U.S. Try to discover the rule that corroborates your answer.

A. *Rule*—States must border the Atlantic Ocean. Correct answers are Connecticut, Delaware, Florida, Georgia, Maine, Maryland, Massachusetts, New Hampshire, New Jersey, New York, North Carolina, Rhode Island, South Carolina, Virginia.

Game 2

Q. Name a country of the world. Try to discover the rule that corroborates your answer.

A. *Rule*—Only the responses of the tallest or blue-eyed or other capriciously designated person are correct, while the responses of all other group members are incorrect.

Game 3

Q. Name animals of the world. Try to discover the rule that corroborates your answer.

A. *Rule*—Only the responses of some capriciously designated person, exclusive of the previous winner, are correct; the responses of all other group members are incorrect.

27

Modified Trust Walk: Experiencing Dependency

Robert L. Bodine and Francis M. Aversano

Goals

    I. To enable the participants to experience dependency in trusting and mistrusting situations.

    II. To encourage the awareness and expression of feelings of trust and mistrust in a dependency situation.

    III. To encourage the awareness and expression of one's responsibility toward peers.

Group Size

    Any number of triads.

Time Required

    Fifty minutes.

Physical Setting

    A large room with seating for all participants and with an area in which a small "S"-shaped maze can be constructed with chairs and/or tables.

Materials

    I. Sufficient blindfolds and lengths of cord or string (each approximately two feet in length) for one-third of the group members.

    II. An instructions card (clearly marked with an A, B, or C) for each member of the triads. (See the Instructions Cards.)

Step-by-Step Process

    I. The facilitator divides the group into triads and gives each member of the triad an A, B, or C instructions card.

II. The facilitator repeats the general instructions to all participants but he omits the distinctions in leader styles. He tells the participants that they will use a cord to lead the blindfolded persons through the maze. The facilitator repeats that the blindfolded person may stop the activity at any time by saying "Stop."

III. After the participants with card A are seated and blindfolded, the facilitator arranges the chairs and/or tables in a simple "S"-shaped maze or some other similar shape. If necessary, the shape of the maze may be changed as the activity progresses.

IV. The facilitator instructs the holders of cards B and C to alternate leading the blindfolded subjects through the maze. The facilitator notes how far each blindfolded person gets in the maze before saying "Stop" and also notes any verbal and nonverbal behavior that is exhibited.

V.   After all participants with card A have been led through the maze, the facilitator leads a discussion focusing on the dependent persons' feelings in a trusting and mistrusting dependency situation. The facilitator provides feedback on his observations during the activity. He may also discuss the following: (1) implementation of the various roles; (2) awareness of feelings while in the maze; (3) feelings while being a leader; (4) feelings while being an observer; (5) trust and mistrust in dependency situations; (6) roadblocks to trust.

Variations

I.   The method of leading the blindfolded, dependent persons may be done with strips of lightweight paper, by hand, or even by verbal directions.

II. Books and other miscellaneous items may be piled or laid on tables and chairs to create sound effects when the participants bump into objects.

III. A short self-assessment may be prepared by the facilitator or the group that focuses on various aspects of anticipated participant reactions.

Notes

The authors have found this activity to be most useful at the completion of other structured experiences that focus on peer cooperation and trusting. It has been successful in the elementary classroom and in both undergraduate and graduate courses.

INSTRUCTIONS CARDS

Card A

Do not show this card to anyone. We are going to experience an activity in trusting. You will be blindfolded and led about the room. You will do this *twice.* You may stop the activity by saying "Stop" and removing your blindfold. Please go to the front of the room and be seated. You will be blindfolded after you are seated. Remember—you can stop the activity at any time by saying "Stop."

Card B

Do not show this card to anyone. We are going to experience an activity in trusting. You will lead a blindfolded group member through a maze. Do not allow the person to hit or bump into anything. You *must* stop when the blindfolded person says "Stop" or when you have completed the full length of the maze.

Card C

Do not show this card to anyone. We are going to experience an activity in trusting. You will lead a blindfolded group member through a maze. Do not cause the person to be injured, but lead him *gently* into the sides of the maze. Do this repeatedly until the person says "Stop" or until you have completed the length of the maze. Remember—*do not cause the person to fall or injure himself.*

28

But That Isn't What You Said: Learning About Deception

Paula K. Horvatich and Gary F. Render

Goals

I. To promote the participants' awareness of their own feelings and the effects of taking an examination when experiencing manipulation and control.

II. To emphasize an understanding of the consequences of breach of promise.

Group Size

The activity is most effective with an ongoing group of no more than thirty participants.

Time Required

Approximately fifty minutes. The instructor announces the exam one class meeting prior to its administration.

Physical Setting

A room in which exams are usually given.

Materials

Copies of an exam unlike the one that the students expect.

Step-by-Step Process

I. The instructor announces to the group that an optional or extra-credit exam will be given at the next class session. He then describes, in some detail, the type of exam (e.g., objective, essay) and the length of the examination.

II. At the next class session, the instructor proceeds in his usual manner of administering an examination. However, he changes the format and length of the exam from what was expected. For example, if the students were informed that the exam would be an objective test, they are given an essay or an oral exam. The new version of the exam should be short enough to allow time for discussion and development of the lesson.

III. The instructor observes and notes the students' verbal and nonverbal reactions to the revised format.

IV. Upon completion of the examination, the instructor questions the students on their feelings about the exam situation, e.g.,
1. Did they enjoy taking the examination?
2. Did they consider it a fair test?
3. Were they bothered by the fact that the exam format and length were different than they had expected?

V. The instructor encourages the students to ask questions and to express their feelings directly concerning the exam situation.

VI. After the students have had ample opportunity to relate their feelings, the instructor explains the purpose underlying the activity.

VII. Then he attempts to facilitate open and honest communication, centering on the students' feelings toward control and manipulation, the effects of the experience on their willingness and ability to take the exam, and the variables involved in their decision to challenge (or not to challenge) the instructor's failure to fulfill his promise.

Variations

I. An activity that emphasizes skills in dealing with control and manipulation may be conducted at the end of this experience.

II. The facilitator may wish to inform participants briefly about the nature of the exam situation prior to conducting the activity. He may even test volunteers only and have nonparticipating persons serve as observers. The negative effects will not be as great.

29

Situation Cards:
A Nonverbal Communication Activity

Al Milliren

Goals

I. To encourage greater accuracy of communication through body movements (actions) and facial expressions.

II. To provide experiences in expressing one's feelings using nonverbal communication.

Group Size

Group size varies. The activity can be conducted with one large group, or several small groups of eight to twelve people can be conducted simultaneously.

Time Required

Time varies according to the repetition of enactments, size of groups, and number of situations included in the session.

Physical Setting

Any large, open area that will accommodate the groups and allow for movement of the participants.

Materials

I. Two or more 3″ x 5″ index cards, with a different nonverbal situation on each card, for each participant. (See Suggested Nonverbal Situation Cards.)

II. Paper and pencils.

Step-by-Step Process

I. The facilitator explains to the participants that they will enact certain situations nonverbally, using body movements and facial expressions. After a person acts out a situation, the remaining group members will try to discover what action was being demonstrated. Individuality of movement and expression is encouraged by the facilitator.

II. The facilitator demonstrates by enacting a particular situation nonverbally. (See Suggested Nonverbal Situation Cards.)

III. He asks the participants to respond verbally to the behaviors they observed in his nonverbal actions. Then he discusses *what* he was trying to communicate.

IV. The facilitator distributes several Nonverbal Situation Cards, paper, and a pencil to each participant. He asks the participants, one at a time, to choose a situation on the card and to act it out in as much detail as possible. He emphasizes that each demonstration should be nonverbal. After each situation is enacted, the observers note all the behaviors involved and guess what was being demonstrated.

V. After each person has demonstrated at least one situation, the facilitator asks the group members to repeat the process, using new situation cards, but this time they are also to show their *feelings* about what they are doing, using facial expressions and body movements. More time is spent on the discussions following each demonstration to help the observers recognize different expressions and movements that show how a person feels about what he is doing.

VI. The facilitator leads a discussion on how feelings are often expressed nonverbally through body movements and facial expressions.

VII. The participants are asked to think of a situation in which they definitely expressed feelings nonverbally, e.g., a happy time or a sad time.

VIII. The facilitator leads a discussion on the similarities and differences among the group members when they express feelings nonverbally.

Variations

I. The demonstration in step II may be given by one of the participants with coaching from the facilitator.

II. If the group is large, smaller groups may be formed to give the participants more opportunities to enact situations and more time to discuss the results.

III. When adults are involved, more time may be spent on enacting situations with feelings. The situations may become increasingly complex and feelings may be expressed more subtly.

IV. This activity may be completed over a two- or three-day period with homework assignments, which may entail having the participants observe family members' nonverbal behaviors.

V. The facilitator may wish to provide another demonstration in step V.

VI. A game can be made of this activity by having the classmates choose sides and try to stump each other by enacting difficult situations.

SUGGESTED NONVERBAL SITUATION CARDS

1. Make a doughnut.
2. Create a pizza.
3. Fry a hamburger.
4. Walk through very deep snow.
5. Carry a full glass of water so as not to spill any.
6. Walk on a carpet of eggs.
7. Play baseball.
8. Play football.
9. Play checkers.
10. Play cards.
11. Ride a bicycle.
12. Skate on ice.
13. Open a large wrapped present.
14. Climb a steep hill.
15. Climb a ladder.
16. Climb a tree.
17. Make and bake cookies.
18. Make and bake a pie.
19. Dry dishes.
20. Set the table.
21. Serve a meal.
22. Move a piano (or any large piece of furniture).
23. Nail some boards together.
24. Put on a pair of boots and buckle them.

30

Group Dynamics:
Awareness of Self and Others

Lois Brooks

Goals

I. To examine group dynamics, such as power structure, leadership behavior, cooperation, motivation, and nonverbal communication.

II. To sensitize the participants to some of their own behaviors within a group setting.

Group Size

From ten to twenty individuals.

Time Required

Forty-five minutes for the activity and thirty minutes for discussion. The task is assigned one class meeting prior to its intended use.

Physical Setting

A classroom with one table per group.

Materials

Glue, string, transparent tape, and masking tape. Table tops may need to be protected.

Step-by-Step Process

I. Prior to the session, the facilitator asks each participant to bring to the next class meeting six objects that have little personal value, e.g., a pencil, an empty spool of thread, a styrofoam cup. The participants are not told what will be done with these objects.

II. At the next meeting, the facilitator asks the participants to place all the objects they have brought to the session in a pile, along with the glue, string, and tape.

111

III. The facilitator selects two individuals to act as barterers. He divides the remaining group members into small groups of three to five persons each.

IV. The facilitator gives the following instructions:
   1. The task of each group is to create a work of art out of the objects in the pile.
   2. During the creating process, group members may *not* communicate with each other verbally or through writing. They may, however, use nonverbal cues, such as gestures and facial expressions.
   3. Each group chooses one individual who (a) is to select eight objects from the pile upon a signal from the facilitator, and (b) may bargain with the barterers for an exchange of objects at any time during the creating process. The representatives may speak with the barterers but *not* with their own groups.

V. The facilitator privately gives the following instructions to the barterers:
   "You are to show preferential treatment to the group representatives; you may reverse your preferential treatment at any time."

VI. The facilitator instructs the groups to begin the building phase. (Thirty minutes.)

VII. After the groups have finished their works of art, the facilitator asks each group to name its creation. (This is done verbally.)

VIII. The facilitator then asks the barterers to judge the best creation (taking its name into consideration), and then to announce their decision.

IX. The facilitator leads a total group discussion on the activity, which may include the following questions:
   1. How many individuals in each group were actively involved in the building process?
   2. Did one person emerge as a leader or did the leadership rotate?
   3. Who influenced the group the most? Least? How?
   4. Who in the group was most motivated to carry the task through to completion?
   5. How well did group members cooperate with one another?
   6. At what point was the frustration level the highest?
   7. How did individual group members feel when trying to communicate nonverbally, particularly when the barterers and the representatives could talk?

8. How did group members communicate with one another?
9. Did the art work gradually evolve or did it completely change shape and direction? Who initiated changes?
10. Did certain objects, such as tape, have premium value?
11. How did group members feel about the selection of objects that their representatives brought back to their groups?
12. How did group representatives feel during the bargaining process when the barterers gave preferential treatment to some of them?
13. How did the barterers feel about the power they were able to wield?
14. What process was used by each group to arrive at a name for its creation?
15. How did group members feel when the barterers announced their selection of the best art work?
16. Was there competition among the groups?
17. What did you learn about your own behavior?

Variations

I. The groups may change representatives at some point during the creating process.

II. The facilitator may announce at the beginning of the session that a prize will be awarded to the best creation.

III. The barterers may be instructed privately to select the "worst" creation for first prize.

IV. The discussion questions may be answered within subgroups.

31

Self-Assessment:
A Focus on Classroom and Small-Group Behavior

Louis Thayer

Goals

I. To encourage learners to assume a larger portion of the responsibility for learning.

II. To help individuals take an active part in examining their own group behavior.

III. To assist the participants in sharing their strengths and weaknesses concerning group behavior in a positive and nonthreatening atmosphere.

Group Size

Any ongoing learning group.

Time Required

Thirty minutes for administration of the instrument; at least thirty to forty-five minutes for the sharing process.

Physical Setting

A classroom in which the group regularly meets.

Materials

I. Pencils.

II. A copy of the Self-Assessment Inventory for each participant.

Step-by-Step Process

I. After the group has met several times, the facilitator administers the Self-Assessment Inventory. (Allow thirty minutes for completion of the instrument.)

II. The facilitator asks the participants to review the instrument and to select three items that they consider personal strengths and three items that they consider personal weaknesses.

III. The facilitator asks the members to divide into subgroups (dyads, triads, or small groups) for a discussion. He encourages each group member to relate his three personal strengths to the group. Other group members are asked to offer feedback to the individual concerning their perceptions or impressions of his strengths.

IV. The facilitator encourages each member to share with his group one or two personal weaknesses. The facilitator asks the group members to respond with care by offering their perceptions or impressions of the stated weaknesses.

V. When the sharing process is completed, the groups assist each member in establishing a goal. Each member is asked to relate one behavioral change that he wishes to work on in other situations. This goal should have much personal value for each individual.

VI. Near the end of the discussion process, the facilitator recommends that the groups refocus on each individual for a minute and relate a strength on which the individual can capitalize.

Variations

I. The instrument may be completed by the participant at home and then brought to the group session for discussion.

II. The facilitator may wish to discuss each person's strengths and weaknesses individually.

III. The facilitator may wish to spend some time developing a group profile with which individuals can compare and contrast their own assessments of group behavior. This comparison can also prove very interesting to the facilitator if he compares different groups.

IV. The statements on the inventory may be discussed one at a time in a large group or in dyads so that members can react to the statements in the presence of another person.

V. The instrument may be used as an observation sheet for noting the interactions of a group in process or of an individual in a group. Feedback may be generated from the observers' tallies and comments on specific items.

VI. The stimulus statements may be used as points of consideration by an individual preparing a personal analysis paper on his behavior in groups.

VII. Participants may be asked to review the statements and to classify them into four or five different categories, such as empathy, genuineness, etc. They could be expected to give reasons for their selection of categories and their placement of items in a category.

VIII. The instrument may be used to involve the participant in a pre- and post-assessment of group behavior when skill training is provided. The facilitator could return the assessment instruments to the participants after training and a post-assessment have been completed.

IX. The participants may ask the facilitator to review the completed instrument during a conference or they may ask him to write responses to each person's self-assessment.

X. The facilitator may ask each person to rate the other participants in his group on selected dimensions. Each person would guess how the other people rated him. A computer analysis can provide interesting and helpful feedback to the participants.

SELF-ASSESSMENT INVENTORY
Louis Thayer

The purpose of this instrument is to help you assess your attitudes and activities during the sessions. Learning is a very personal process and, consequently, the learner should play an important role in the assessment of his own learning. An honest response to each statement may be the first step in allowing this instrument to help you reflect on your activities and learning.

Directions: Circle the number from 1 to 5 that best represents your response to each statement, based on the following:

1 means "never," "not at all."

2 means "somewhat," "sometimes," "rarely," "a little."

3 means "about as often as not," "an average amount."

4 means "usually," "a good deal," "frequently."

5 means "regularly," "practically always," "entirely."

In the space provided for comments after the scoring of each statement, try to write one or two of your perceptions on your group behavior and your attitudes as they relate to the stimulus statements. Try to clarify your own scoring.

1. I defend my ideas vehemently, disregarding the opinions of others.

    Never   1   2   3   4   5   Regularly

    Comments: _____

2. I encourage others to express their feelings and ideas on discussion topics.

    Never   1   2   3   4   5   Regularly

    Comments: _____

3. I believe that learning is my own responsibility.

    Never   1   2   3   4   5   Regularly

    Comments: _____

4. I respond in a genuine and honest manner to peers and the facilitator.

   Never   1   2   3   4   5   Regularly

   Comments: _____

5. I share personal feelings and experiences with the learning group.

   Never   1   2   3   4   5   Regularly

   Comments: _____

6. I respect the feelings of others.

   Never   1   2   3   4   5   Regularly

   Comments: _____

7. I am sensitive to the feelings of others.

   Never   1   2   3   4   5   Regularly

   Comments: _____

8. I recognize nonverbal cues that communicate various emotions.

   Never   1   2   3   4   5   Regularly

   Comments: _____

9. I offer constructive feedback when I disagree with the views of others.

   Never   1   2   3   4   5   Regularly

   Comments: _____

10. I defend a person who is being criticized.

   Never   1   2   3   4   5   Regularly

   Comments: _____

11. I expose indirect criticism when others do not recognize it.

   Never   1   2   3   4   5   Regularly

   Comments: _____

12. I seek feedback and clarification on the effects of my behavior, attitudes, and values.

    Never   1   2   3   4   5   Regularly

    Comments: _____

13. I display hostility when things don't go my way.

    Never   1   2   3   4   5   Regularly

    Comments: _____

14. I expect to have the last word in an exchange of views.

    Never   1   2   3   4   5   Regularly

    Comments: _____

15. I find it necessary to understand and to change some of my attitudes,
values, and behaviors.

    Never   1   2   3   4   5   Regularly

    Comments: _____

16. I feel comfortable in responding to the facilitator when I am in conflict with his views or don't understand them.

    Never   1   2   3   4   5   Regularly

    Comments: _____

17. I set aside appropriate amounts of time to spend on projects of interest to me.

    Never   1   2   3   4   5   Regularly

    Comments: _____

18. I demonstrate empathy by understanding what another person is
saying and I communicate to him what it is that I understand.

    Never   1   2   3   4   5   Regularly

    Comments: _____

19. I avoid conflicts or disagreements that arise in the group.

    Never   1   2   3   4   5   Regularly

    Comments: _____

20. I rely on others to help me establish my goals and values.

   Never   1   2   3   4   5   Regularly

   Comments:_____

21. I am aware of the role that I play in small-group interaction.

   Never   1   2   3   4   5   Regularly

   Comments:_____

22. I value the process of learning more than any specific content vehicle.

   Never   1   2   3   4   5   Regularly

   Comments:_____

23. I feel threatened when exercises are provided for self-assessment.

   Never   1   2   3   4   5   Regularly

   Comments:_____

24. I depend on others to direct my group behavior and my teaching-learning style.

   Never   1   2   3   4   5   Regularly

   Comments:_____

25. I prefer to be a passive learner rather than an active, participating learner.

   Never   1   2   3   4   5   Regularly

   Comments:_____

32

Examining Stereotypes: A Data-Based Group Process for Helping Professionals

Bruce J. Yasgur and Thomas H. Hawkes

Goals

I. To help the participants overcome their often-stereotyped conceptions of people who live in the inner city.

II. To increase the participants' sensitivity to the social-emotional needs of the individuals they help.

Group Size

Group size can vary. The activity has been used effectively with ten to forty participants, consisting of students or workers in urban helping professions.

Time Required

Approximately three hours. The activity may be divided into several sessions.

Physical Setting

Any room large enough to accommodate the participants.

Materials

I. Pencils or pens.

II. Chalkboard and chalk or newsprint and a felt-tipped marker.

III. A copy of the Examining Stereotypes Instructions Sheet for each participant.

IV. Two copies of the Examining Stereotypes Predictions Sheet for each participant.

V. A copy of the Examining Stereotypes Role-Play Sheet.

VI. A copy of the Examining Stereotypes Research Data Sheet for each participant.

Step-by-Step Process

I. The facilitator distributes pencils, an Examining Stereotypes Instructions Sheet, and one copy of the Examining Stereotypes Predictions Sheet to each participant. He reviews the directions and answers any questions.

II. When the participants have completed the predictions sheet, the facilitator records the group's predictions for each question on the chalkboard by a show-of-hands procedure.

III. The facilitator asks the participants to discuss reasons (assumptions) for their predictions. He then summarizes and points out disparities in assumptions or hypotheses. The participants will recognize that their predictions and reasons vary widely and that each person operates on assumptions that reflect his own history and preconceptions.

IV. The facilitator chooses two participants to play each character in the role play (see the Examining Stereotypes Role-Play Sheet) and selects one participant to serve as the teacher, counselor, or principal in each role-play situation. The role players begin the role play. (Twenty minutes per role play.)

V. The facilitator leads a discussion on the differences between portrayed self and hidden self.

VI. The facilitator distributes another Examining Stereotypes Predictions Sheet to each person, allowing sufficient time for the participants to complete the instrument. He then records the revised predictions on the chalkboard next to the original ones. The facilitator asks the participants who changed their predictions to share the reasons for the changes.

VII. The facilitator gives each participant a copy of the Examining Stereotypes Research Data Sheet and continues the discussion, emphasizing the need for the participants to recognize their own stereotypes and assumptions about themselves and others before they can offer professional help.

Variations

I. If time is limited, the facilitator can shorten the list of items on the predictions sheet to statements that represent different concerns (real danger, wounded emotions, achievement, etc.) as well as a lie-scale item ("Do you ever worry?").

II. A small-group discussion on how people use "covers" to hide true feelings could be substituted for the role play.

III. The role play could be performed in small-group settings, with each participant in a role, or the audience could suggest alter-ego roles to the actors after observing the "up-front" interaction.

Commentary

Several variations of this activity have been conducted by the authors with a number of education and psychology classes at Temple University and at the Community College of Philadelphia with teachers, counselors, and management personnel from several public agencies. The initial scores (number of correct predictions out of sixteen items) usually range from 5 to 7 on the average, regardless of the group's background, mean age, etc.

The original investigations of children's worries using the General Anxiety Questionnaire (GAQ) were conducted by Hawkes and Koff (1970) and by Hawkes and Furst (1971). Hawkes and Furst (1973) also conducted the initial study in which students and teachers were asked to predict how children from differing backgrounds responded to GAQ items.

In an extensive follow-up study, Yasgur and Carner (1973) reported that not only did inner-city children worry with greater quantity than did their more privileged counterparts, but that they were far more worried about survival. For example, an accident to an inner-city child often meant being physically harmed or killed; to an outer-city child it usually meant getting a dent in the car or, at worst, falling off a bicycle.

References

Hawkes, T. H., & Furst, N. F. Research note: Race, SES, achievement, IQ, and teacher rating of students' behavior as factors relating to anxiety in upper elementary school children. *Sociology of Education,* 1971, 44(3), 333-350.

Hawkes, T. H., & Furst, N. F. An investigation of the (mis) conceptions of pre- and inservice teachers as to the manifestation of anxiety in upper elementary school children from different racial-SES backgrounds. *Psychology in the Schools,* 1973, 10(1), 23-32.

Hawkes, T. H., & Koff, R. Differences in anxiety of private school and inner city public elementary school children. *Psychology in the Schools,* 1970, 7(3), 250-259.

Yasgur, B., & Carner, E. *An investigation of the degree and nature of anxiety in children from different SES and racial backgrounds, and some implications for the schools.* Presented at the American Educational Research Associations' Annual Conference, February 1973 (a). ERIC #ED 074 164.

EXAMINING STEREOTYPES INSTRUCTIONS SHEET*

Many of us operate from different theoretical frameworks. It is often interesting to see differences, if any, that exist in any one group.

You are going to be asked to hypothesize how you think children from two different backgrounds responded to sixteen items taken from the General Anxiety Questionnaire (Hawkes & Koff, 1970), an instrument designed to measure worrying.

One group of children was composed of two hundred black fifth and sixth graders in an inner-city ghetto school. The school, which was characterized by a high turnover rate in school population (30 percent in and 30 percent out), had an exceedingly high rate of children who were on welfare. The children's average I.Q. was 93.

The second group of children consisted of two hundred fifth- and sixth-grade pupils in a private school. The children in this school came from predominantly professional homes. Ninety percent of the children were white, 5 percent black, and 5 percent Oriental. Their average I.Q. was 132. This population was quite analogous to an upper-middle-class suburban school in terms of academic outlook and culture.

Directions:
a. Please read each item carefully.
b. If you think more inner-city children answered "Yes" to the question, check the first column. If you think more private-school children answered "Yes," check the second column. If you think that the responses were relatively the *same* (within 10 percent for *each* group), check the third column.
c. After you have made your decision, give a very brief reason for your answer.

---

*Adapted from Hawkes and Furst (1973).

EXAMINING STEREOTYPES PREDICTIONS SHEET*

Directions: Place a check mark in column A if you think more inner-city students answered "Yes" to the question, in column B if you think more private-school students answered "Yes," and in column C if you think the responses were roughly the same (within 10 percent).

	A Inner City	B Private School	C Same
1. Do you worry that you might get hurt in an accident? Reason:			
2. I feel I have to be best in everything. Reason:			
3. Do you ever worry? Reason:			
4. I have worried about things that did not really make any difference. Reason:			
5. Others seem to do things easier than I can. Reason:			

*From Hawkes and Furst (1973).

	A Inner City	B Private School	C Same
6. I worry about how well I am doing in school. Reason:			
7. I am afraid of the dark. Reason:			
8. Do you think you worry more than other boys and girls? Reason:			
9. Has anyone ever been able to scare you? Reason:			
10. I have bad dreams. Reason:			
11. I often worry about what could happen to my parents. Reason:			
12. I wish I could be very far from here. Reason:			
13. It is hard for me to keep my mind on my schoolwork. Reason:			

	A Inner City	B Private School	C Same
14. My feelings get hurt easily when I am scolded. Reason:			
15. I feel that others do not like the way I do things. Reason:			
16. I worry most of the time. Reason:			

EXAMINING STEREOTYPES ROLE-PLAY SHEET*

The following character sketches can be introduced in the role-play component of this activity. The roles are based on suggestions of black, inner-city residents and former gang members who participated in an earlier version of this activity. These roles can be revised or expanded and/or new characters can be added, e.g., a preteen student, a social worker, a school principal, a counselor, a policeman, a politician.

In preparing other roles, follow the guideline that most people try to appear poised and confident in public, while harboring worries and insecurities that they are loathe to admit. Minority-group members who live in substandard living conditions seem to have more worries and insecurities, including a genuine concern for safety and survival, than those who are more privileged (Yasgur & Carner, 1973).

Directions:
1. Choose two participants to play each character in the role play. One person, who remains seated, portrays the character as he outwardly appears to others. The other person, who stands behind his alter ego, portrays the inner, hidden character. Select one participant to play the teacher, counselor, or principal in each situation.
2. The role players should be given some time to familiarize themselves with their parts (optional).
3. Establish a problem (scene) and set the stage for the role play, e.g., a conference with the teacher, counselor, or principal.
4. The role play is a conference between the teacher, counselor, or principal and one of the following characters. During the role play, the hidden self speaks after the portrayed self in each interaction.

Sample Roles

Role 1—Gang Member

Portrayed Self: "I'm tops and I'm tough! Ain't no teacher or pig or nobody gonna tell me how to act. . . ."
Hidden Self: "Good thing I got my corner boys, otherwise I wouldn't have nobody. I'd be scared to walk down the street, let alone come to school. . . ."

---

*Both the portrayed and the hidden roles of the gang member, girl friend, and mother were based on suggestions of, and initially enacted by, black, inner-city residents, including former gang members.

Our appreciation is extended to Ms. Angela Russo, of ACTION, and Mr. Erv Morris, of JACS, for their help in developing the role-play component.

Role 2—Girl Friend

Portrayed Self: "You don't mess with me, 'cause my boyfriend and his brothers will tear you up!"

Hidden Self: "Without him I'd be nobody. I better keep doin' just what he wants so he don't leave me. . . ."

Role 3—His Mother

Portrayed Self: "I always did the best for him, and he listens to his mother. . . ."

Hidden Self: "I'm so ashamed that these people are always tellin' me what a poor mother I've been. But they kept me always from my kids watchin' theirs and keepin' their houses clean. If I didn't go out and get drunk every night I'd kill myself. . . ."

Role 4—Teacher

Portrayed Self: "I've done the best I can to teach these kids, despite an almost total lack of support from the parents or the educational system. . . ."

Hidden Self: "How can I admit that I haven't really tried? It's just so much work and I can't keep up with it. I feel guilty, but all I want to do anymore is collect my paycheck. . . ."

EXAMINING STEREOTYPES RESEARCH DATA SHEET*

The following data present the percentage of black, inner-city children and white, private-school children (5th and 6th graders) who responded "Yes" to sixteen of the fifty GAQ items.

	Black Inner City	White Private School
1. Do you worry that you might get hurt in some accident?	77	30
2. I feel I have to be best in everything.	42	23
3. Do you ever worry?	84	88
4. I have worried about things that did not really make any difference.	45	63
5. Others seem to do things easier than I do.	59	44
6. I worry about how well I am doing in school.	87	66
7. I am afraid of the dark.	46	15
8. Do you think you worry more than other boys and girls?	28	21
9. Has anyone ever been able to scare you?	80	78
10. I have bad dreams.	55	35
11. I often worry about what could happen to my parents.	91	60
12. I wish I could be very far from here.	54	19
13. It is hard for me to keep my mind on my schoolwork.	40	18
14. My feelings get hurt easily when I am scolded.	66	41
15. I feel that others do not like the way I do things.	54	30
16. I worry most of the time.	32	11

---

*These data, reported by Hawkes and Koff (1970), were corroborated by the results of a similar study conducted by Hawkes and Furst (1971).

33

Work-Related Concepts: Increasing Personal Awareness

Cheng C. Liu

Goals

I. To orient participants to empirically derived work-related concepts.

II. To increase the participants' awareness of work environments.

III. To provide an opportunity for the participants to evaluate their feelings and perceptions about work and to share these feelings with other group members.

IV. To provide attitudinal information for curricular and instructional development.

Group Size

Any number of students. The activity is most suited for students in grades nine through twelve and for post-secondary students. It is also suitable for vocational-technical education students and manpower program and vocational rehabilitation trainees.

Time Required

Time requirements vary depending on the number of work-related concepts and the form of instruments used.

Physical Setting

A classroom in which the group regularly meets or any setting in which desks and chairs are available. (A quiet surrounding is preferred.)

Materials

I. One Work-Related Concepts "booklet" for each participant. The booklet should be prepared in such a way that each work-related concept appears on a separate page. (See the Instructions for Preparing the Work-Related Concepts Booklet.)

II. Pencils or pens.

III. A stop watch or a watch with a second hand.

Step-by-Step Process

I. The facilitator tells the participants that they will have an opportunity to express their feelings and perceptions about some aspects of the work environment.

II. He distributes copies of the Work-Related Concepts Booklet and reviews the instructions sheet. The facilitator reminds the participants of the time limitations on each form of booklet.

III. Upon a signal from the facilitator, the participants begin to work on the first worksheet. The facilitator stops the process after the allotted time period.

IV. The participants are instructed to go on to the next worksheet when instructed by the facilitator.

V. The process continues until the participants finish each page of their booklets.

VI. The facilitator divides the participants into small groups. They are instructed to read their responses to the group and to discuss their feelings and perceptions as compared with other group members. The facilitator serves as a moderator and resource person in the group discussion.

VII. The facilitator summarizes the discussion of each work-related concept with the total group. Further case study may be assigned to the group after the discussion.

VIII. The facilitator collects the booklets and continues analyzing the responses made by the group members. He can report the results at a later date.

Variations

I. If the facilitator wishes to score the responses, a detailed scoring procedure with computer programs is available from the contributor or from sources listed in the References.

II. For elementary or special-education students, the work-related concepts can be prerecorded and played back to the participants. In this manner, the responses may be oral instead of written.

III. The number of bipolar adjective scales in Form A may be reduced to suit the individual user's situation (taking into consideration the participants' age, background, and educational level).

Notes

Numerous educators and researchers are becoming increasingly aware that the affective dimensions of human development must be accounted for in career education. Public schools, as well as vocational education programs, have traditionally concentrated on the development of cognitive skills while ignoring total development. However, students are now being recognized as whole persons with a broad spectrum of developmental needs, including both cognitive and affective aspects.

These self-reporting instruments were designed to provide the instructor with information for developing instructional materials relating to attitudes. They can be used as a form of pre- and/or post-assessment for instruction relating to work attitudes.

Techniques and procedures used to analyze a large group's responses are available by writing to the contributor or by referring to the references listed below.

References

Essex, D. W., & Liu, C. C. A methodology to assess the content and structure of affective and descriptive meanings associated with the work environment. Columbus: The Center for Vocational Education, Ohio State University, December 1974. (a) For sale by the Superintendent of Documents, U.S. Government Printing Office, Washington, D.C. 20402.

Essex, D. W., & Liu, C. C. Toward the development of a work-related semantic differential using word association procedures: A source unit for bipolar scales. Columbus: The Center for Vocational Education, Ohio State University, April 1974. (Draft) (b)

INSTRUCTIONS FOR PREPARING
THE WORK-RELATED CONCEPTS BOOKLET

1. Chose the work-related concepts (e.g., my job, my job security, my pay, my working conditions, my supervisor, my company policies, my co-workers) that you wish to use from the Suggested List of Work-Related Concepts.

2. Decide which instrument format—Form A or Form B—to use to present the concepts to the participants.

   On Form A, the participants record their impressions of different work-related concepts by rating them on a scale. The Form A booklet should contain an Instructions Sheet for Form A and a separate worksheet listing each concept to be rated. Each worksheet in Form A requires three minutes of response time.

   On Form B, the participants write different words that come to mind when they think of a key concept. The Form B booklet should contain an Instructions Sheet for Form B and a separate worksheet listing each concept. Each worksheet in Form B requires one minute of response time for each work-related concept.

3. Prepare a booklet for each participant based on the instructions above. List the concept to be rated or responded to in the blank at the top of each worksheet for Forms A and B.

SUGGESTED LIST OF WORK-RELATED CONCEPTS*

The work-related concepts on the following page are categorized into several sections. Any number of concepts can be selected. Please consider the age, background, and educational level of the participants in your selection of concepts.

---

*From D. W. Essex & C. C. Liu, *A Methodology to Assess the Content and Structure of Affective and Descriptive Meanings Associated with a Work Environment.* Columbus: The Center for Vocational Education, Ohio State University, December 1974.

Job Content	General Need Satisfaction	Compensation	Working Conditions	Supervision	Company and Union	Co-Workers
Assignment and perceived complexity of tasks	*Security*	My pay	My working conditions	My supervisor	Company policies of my job	My fellow co-workers
My opportunities to do a variety of tasks	My job security	My opportunities for promotion	The work methods used on my job	My supervisor's ability to handle people	Handling of grievances on my job	
Opportunities to do challenging work	*Social*	My fringe benefits	The work pace used on my job	Interaction with my supervisor	The union on my job	
My job	Interaction with my co-workers		My working hours	Supervisor's evaluation of my work		
Control of work methods and work pace	Opportunities to help others in the community		The equipment used on my job			
My control over work methods	Me at work		Overtime work			
My control over work pace	*Esteem*		Coffee breaks			
Interference with my job	Moral "rightness" of my job					
Skills and abilities of worker	Recognition of my work					
Use of my abilities at work	My prestige at work					
My competence at work	Prestige of my job in the community					
Opportunities for on-the-job training	*Autonomy*					
	Freedom to use my own judgment at work					
	My self-confidence at work					
	Self-actualization					
	Opportunities for self-fulfillment					
	Feeling of accomplishment at work					
	Daydreaming at work					

INSTRUCTIONS SHEET FOR FORM A

Directions: On each page of the booklet, you will find a *different* concept to be judged. Beneath the concept are a list of adjectives and a set of scales. Make a check mark along the scale to indicate how you rate the concept.

Examples:

If you feel that the concept at the top of the page is **highly related** to one end of the scale, e.g., fair or unfair, place your check mark as follows:

fair <u>X</u>:__:__:__:__:__ unfair   or   fair __:__:__:__:__:<u>X</u> unfair

If you feel that the concept is **closely related** to one or the other end of the scale, place your check mark as follows:

fair __:<u>X</u>:__:__:__:__ unfair   or   fair __:__:__:__:<u>X</u>:__ unfair

If the concept seems only **slightly related** to one side of the scale (as opposed to the other side), place your check mark as follows:

fair __:__:<u>X</u>:__:__:__ unfair   or   fair __:__:__:__:<u>X</u>:__ unfair

If the concept appears to be **neutral** on the scale (i.e., both sides of the scale seem equally associated with the concept), or if the scale is *completely irrelevant* or *unrelated* to the concept, place your check mark in the middle space.

fair __:__:__:<u>X</u>:__:__:__ unfair

The direction toward which you check, of course, depends on which of the two ends of the scale seems more characteristic of the concept you are judging.

Note

a. Place your check mark in the middle of the spaces, not on the boundaries, i.e.,

__:__:<u>X</u>:__:__:__   *not*   __:__:**X**:__:__:__

b. Be sure that you check every scale for each concept—do not skip any.

c. Never put more than one check mark on a single scale.

Do not spend more than a few seconds marking each scale. On the other hand, do not be careless, because we want to analyze your true impressions. Mark each concept independently and do not look back and forth between concepts. Your first impression is what counts.

You will have three minutes to respond to each work-related concept. Please do not turn the page until you are instructed by the facilitator.

FORM A

Work-Related Concept: _____

incompatible	__:__:__:__:__:__	compatible
thoughtful	__:__:__:__:__:__	thoughtless
good	__:__:__:__:__:__	bad
unreasonable	__:__:__:__:__:__	reasonable
unfair	__:__:__:__:__:__	fair
harmful	__:__:__:__:__:__	helpful
vague	__:__:__:__:__:__	precise
unsuccessful	__:__:__:__:__:__	successful
abstract	__:__:__:__:__:__	concrete
active	__:__:__:__:__:__	passive
interesting	__:__:__:__:__:__	boring
hectic	__:__:__:__:__:__	calm
infrequent	__:__:__:__:__:__	frequent
relaxed	__:__:__:__:__:__	tense
familiar	__:__:__:__:__:__	strange
careless	__:__:__:__:__:__	careful
easy	__:__:__:__:__:__	difficult
cautious	__:__:__:__:__:__	rash
varied	__:__:__:__:__:__	routine
discouraging	__:__:__:__:__:__	encouraging
insecure	__:__:__:__:__:__	secure
safe	__:__:__:__:__:__	dangerous
stable	__:__:__:__:__:__	changeable
clean	__:__:__:__:__:__	dirty
unnecessary	__:__:__:__:__:__	necessary
efficient	__:__:__:__:__:__	inefficient
sufficient	__:__:__:__:__:__	insufficient
impractical	__:__:__:__:__:__	practical
unimportant	__:__:__:__:__:__	important
powerful	__:__:__:__:__:__	powerless

INSTRUCTIONS SHEET FOR FORM B

Directions: As you consider each work-related concept on the following pages, try to fill in all fifteen blanks by writing as many different responses for each key concept as you can. Try to write all the responses that will best indicate what the key concept means to you within one minute's responding time (for each page).

Example: In the spaces provided below, someone has written different words that came to *his* mind as he looked at the key concept. All his responses are different, they are single words, and they were his first impressions of the concept.

Work-Related Concept: **Job Knowledge**

1. *Experience*
2. *Skill*
3. *Ability*
4. *Necessary*
5. *Training*
6. *Helpful*
7. *Performance*
8. _____
9. _____
10. _____
11. _____
12. _____
13. _____
14. _____
15. _____

Note: It is not necessary for you to fill in all fifteen blanks or to try to write as many different kinds of responses for each key concept as the person did for "job knowledge." However, you should try to write all those responses that will best describe what the key concept means to you. You will have one minute to respond to each concept. Please do not turn the page until instructed by the facilitator.

FORM B

Work-Related Concept: _____

1. _____

2. _____

3. _____

4. _____

5. _____

6. _____

7. _____

8. _____

9. _____

10. _____

11. _____

12. _____

13. _____

14. _____

15. _____

34

HFFT:
Heller's Forced-Feedback Technique

Steven A. Heller

Goals

I. To encourage the development of increased open feedback through facilitator feedback.

II. To provide feedback to those group members who normally inhibit feedback and effective communication.

Group Size

At least twenty-five persons who normally interact with each other. A large group insures anonymity of members during the feedback process.

Time Required

Approximately two hours. Additional time may be needed for processing feelings and/or tension-reducing activities.

Physical Setting

A carpeted, open-space room with good acoustics and no physical barriers between group members.

Materials

I. Three 3″ x 5″ lined index cards and a pencil or pen for each participant.

II. Chalkboard and chalk.

Step-by-Step Process

I. The facilitator begins by discussing how open communication is essential for problem resolution and effective team functioning and points out the need for a process in which feedback about attitudes and behaviors can be shared openly. He suggests that some group members may discover data about themselves and their communication styles of which they may be unaware. He also discusses the risks involved in the open feedback of this activity.

II. The group decides whether they should begin a feedback process that is anonymous or whether a different sort of confronting or open-feedback process should be used.

III. If the group chooses a feedback process in which the members initially remain anonymous, the facilitator starts the activity by examining and discussing constructive feedback principles. (See "On Using Structured Experiences.")

IV. The facilitator distributes pencils and three index cards to each participant.

V. He reemphasizes the principles of constructive feedback and gives the following instructions, allowing sufficient time for the participants to write each response.
1. On the upper left-hand side of *each* index card, please write the name of *one* person in this group with whom you find it difficult to communicate. A different person should be indicated on each card.
2. Rank-order the three names by writing the number 1 by the name of the person with whom you have the most difficulty communicating, 2 by the second most, and 3 by the third most.
3. On the *second* line of each card, describe what it is that you would like to communicate to that person either now or at any other time.
4. On the *fourth* line of each index card, describe how you feel when you try to communicate with that person.
5. On the *sixth* line of each card, please describe what the person does (i.e., his behavior) that inhibits your communication with him.

VI. The facilitator collects the index cards, sorts them by name, and tallies the number of times that each individual was mentioned by the group.

VII. The facilitator distributes the cards to the members who are named on the cards. He also shares the frequency counts with the group without mentioning names, i.e., someone in this group received fifteen cards, another received eight, etc.

VIII. Members who have received cards are asked to share the general nature of the feedback that they received on the second line of the card. At all times, the facilitator keeps the process constructive and relates individual concerns to the goal of better group functioning.

IX. The facilitator continues the processing of lines four and six from the cards. When members feel comfortable enough, they are encouraged to *own* the feedback that they shared anonymously. The facilitator models understanding and listening behaviors as he facilitates the feedback exchange.

X. Although the processing of the anonymous feedback may not be complete, the facilitator begins to show the links between good communication and effective group functioning. He also encourages the process of more *open* communication and constructive feedback.

XI. The facilitator and the group decide how the feedback process, the focus on better communication, and the group's functioning will be continued at the next group session.

Variations

I. The facilitator may wish to include positive feedback aspects as a component in step V.

II. The facilitator may wish to turn step III into a full-scale training activity on how to give negative feedback.

III. After step V, the facilitator may wish to help the participants talk about some of their feelings after writing down their feedback on cards.

IV. The feedback process may be accomplished without cards; however, the members will have to *own* their feedback responses.

V. A smaller group size may be used with less chance of anonymity.

VI. The facilitator may use blank cards so that every member gets at least two cards. However, this can detract from the possible fact that only a small number of individuals are negatively affecting the group's functioning.

Notes

This structured experience should be used with extreme care. Extensive amounts of negative feedback can harm an individual's emotional health and affect his functioning in a group for many sessions.

The activity has been used in a number of organization development workshops that focus on existing interpersonal problems. The technique provides (1) information to the nonreceptive members about the problems that other participants encounter when providing them with meaningful feedback, and (2) information to the total group regarding the extent of the communication problem.

This activity may also be used with groups or organizations that have special problems in feedback and open communication. However, a very competent facilitator should be present to aid in the processing of feedback. Adequate time for processing should be available or the activity should *not* be attempted.

35

Negative Feedback:
A Training Experience

Connie Farnham Kravas and Konstantinos J. Kravas

Goals

I. To help the participants recognize that open and honest communication often necessitates the sharing of negative feedback.

II. To assist the participants in identifying personal feelings and concerns about giving and receiving negative feedback.

III. To provide training for the participants in sharing negative perceptions in an open yet sensitive manner, thus allowing the recipient to "hear" the message, rather than to assume a defensive posture.

Group Size

Any number of triads.

Time Required

Approximately two hours.

Physical Setting

A comfortable room in which the triads can interact.

Materials

Paper and a pencil for each participant.

Step-by-Step Process

I. The facilitator distributes the pencils and paper and asks the participants to form triads.

II. He provides the following directions, allowing time for the participants to consider their responses to each question.

"Take a few minutes to recall the last time someone gave you negative feedback. Try to identify the feelings that you experienced when this information was shared with you. [Pause] Did it seem personally threatening? What verbal and nonverbal responses did you make to the person who shared this negative feedback with you? [Pause] As you reflect on this situation, in what ways were your responses effective or ineffective? Were you comfortable or uncomfortable with the responses you made? After you have thought about this incident for a few minutes, describe the situation and your related feelings as fully as possible."

III. Once the participants have completed their written anecdotes, the facilitator asks the members of each triad to share their feelings, attitudes, and behaviors related to their real experiences in giving and receiving negative feedback.

IV. During the discussions, the facilitator helps the group members focus on effective and ineffective principles of giving and receiving feedback. (See the Effective Feedback Principles Sheet.)

V. Following the discussion, the facilitator asks the members of each triad to exchange their papers, which will be used as immediate material for the sharing of negative feedback via realistic simulations between the triad members. In each triad, one of the participants, the "giver," uses the content of the "receiver's" episode to give the receiver negative feedback in the here-and-now. Utilizing the principles of effective feedback, the giver interacts with the receiver and attempts honestly to share the feedback with him. The third person, the "process-observer," carefully observes and assesses the dynamics of the interaction.

VI. After several minutes, members of the triad discuss the dynamics of the interactive experience. The process-observer shares data manifested by both the giver and the receiver during the exchange.

VII. The triads continue the simulated experience until each member has experienced the part of the giver, the receiver, and the process-observer.

VIII. The facilitator reassembles the large group to discuss the triad experiences, the feedback principles, and the setting of behavioral change goals related to giving and receiving negative feedback.

Variations

I. The facilitator may wish to demonstrate a role-playing situation with one triad group and to involve the large group in a discussion of the role play.

II. If videotape equipment is available, the facilitator could record two or three of the simulated sessions for playback during the discussion session to examine effective and ineffective behaviors.

III. Before the learning group arrives, the facilitator may wish to videotape a simulated situation on feedback for use in modeling appropriate and inappropriate behaviors.

Notes

There may be a tendency for the participants in this activity to role-play their responses, rather than to interact openly in the here-and-now. The facilitator should encourage them to respond as genuinely as possible in the here-and-now. For example, the receiver should not necessarily respond to the negative feedback in the same way that he did during the previous experience. The giver, likewise, should actually give the feedback, rather than communicate that "I'm just pretending."

EFFECTIVE FEEDBACK PRINCIPLES SHEET

Giving Feedback

To be maximally useful to the recipient, feedback should be:

1. Given in such a way that the receiver can "hear" the message. This requires that the giver communicate that he cares about and wants to help the recipient.
2. Given directly and with real feeling, and based on a trusting relationship between the giver and the receiver.
3. Descriptive of the behavior of the receiver and of the effects of his behavior. Feedback should not threaten or judge what he *is* as a person.
4. Specific rather than general, utilizing clear examples to describe the behavior.
5. Timely—given at a time when the receiver might be able to listen to and receive it.
6. Inclusive only of behaviors that the receiver might be able to change.

Receiving Feedback

When receiving feedback, the individual should:

1. Make an effort to listen to the giver with an open mind—to "hear" the message rather than to react defensively.
2. Remember that the feedback represents the perceptions only of the giver. Feedback should be elicited from other individuals to determine if they support the validity of someone else's perceptions.
3. Seek as many possible examples of the behavior as possible.

36

Frustration: A Feedback Activity

David L. Donahue

Goals

I. To help the participants become aware of their responses to frustrating situations.

II. To enable the participants to observe forms of nonverbal behavior exhibited by frustrated/uneasy listeners.

Group Size

Any number of triads.

Time Required

One hour.

Physical Setting

A large room (or several rooms) in which the triads are separated from each other by at least fifteen feet.

Materials

I. A copy of the appropriate Instructions Sheet for each A, B, and C participant.

II. Chalkboard and chalk.

III. Paper and pencils.

Step-by-Step Process

I. The facilitator asks the participants to form triads.

II. He asks each triad to select a member to play participant A, B, and C.

III. The facilitator temporarily segregates all participants according to their A, B, and C function. He distributes their appropriate Instructions Sheets and offers a brief question-and-answer session about their directions. When he speaks with the A participants, the facilitator suggests a list of possible topics to discuss in the triads. He gives the C participants paper and pencils to make notes. Participants are instructed *not* to show their directions to other members of their triad.

IV. The participants return to their original triads and begin the process according to their instructions. The process proceeds for a minimum of two minutes to a maximum of ten minutes.

V. Upon completion of the designated time period, the participants again form groups according to their A, B, and C function. The facilitator asks the members of each group to share their perceptions, feelings, thoughts, and observations about the process in the triads. Each group receives pencils and paper in order to make a list of the feelings related by its individual members. (This discussion lasts approximately ten minutes.)

VI. The facilitator reassembles the subgroups into one large group.

VII. He asks the A participants to list their behaviors during the triad activity. (All participants may respond to the list.) Then the B participants are asked to list their feelings and perceptions concerning the triad process. Then the C participants offer their observations of the nonverbal behaviors. Both A and B participants are asked about the effects of the evaluative statements in their directions.

VIII. The facilitator explores the feelings that the B participants experienced and discusses other situations in which they have experienced the same feelings.

IX. The facilitator leads a discussion on some of the causes of frustration in communication, how perceptions are affected by frustration, how people react when frustrated, how one handles frustration, and how one causes frustration.

X. Then the facilitator asks the participants to name groups of people or individuals who exhibit behaviors like the A participants, the B participants, and the C participants. The facilitator helps them make comparisons between professions or various groups of people.

Variations

I. The list of topics chosen by the A participants can vary considerably in content focus. The items should reflect the common interest of the group and should be ones about which participants can easily converse.

II. Instead of using triads for the activity, small groups of six each may be formed. The directions would remain essentially the same, but there would be two A participants, two B participants, and two C participants. (Or, alternatively, there may be two A participants, one B participant, and three C participants.)

III. This structured experience may be followed by an activity that helps participants deal with frustration and avoid causing frustration in communication.

FRUSTRATION INSTRUCTIONS SHEET

Participant A

Tasks:

A. Your function in the triad is to relate your point of view on one of the topics suggested by the facilitator. Speak continuously in a normal tone of voice for at least two to ten minutes. You are *not* to answer questions! When questions are asked, you may either nod or ignore the question completely. Remember, you are to speak continuously for the allotted time period.

B. The function of participant B is to break your train of thought and to stall for time.

C. The function of participant C is to *grade* you, based on the following criteria:
   1. Did you speak for the full time?
   2. Did you speak clearly?
   3. Was participant B able to stop you? Did you answer questions?

Note:

Remember, participant A, you are being graded!

Participant B

Tasks:

A. While participant A speaks on one of the topics, your function is to ask him questions. You may ask clarification questions or you may ask questions of logic. You *must* stop participant A and make him clarify his position because you may be selected to restate his point of view to the group.

B. The function of participant A is to explain his point of view. He is to make that perfectly clear to you by responding to your questions.

C. The function of participant C is to observe you. He will note the frequency and quality of questions that you ask and the explanations you receive from participant A. *If the explanation is not clear, you will not receive credit for the question.*

Note:

Remember, participant B, you are being graded!

Participant C

Tasks:

You are an observer. Make sure that participants A and B are directly facing each other and are no more than four feet apart. You are to place yourself an equal distance from each and far enough to the side so that neither can see what you are writing. During the triad interaction, note the nonverbal behavior exhibited by both participants. When one smiles or nods, for example, take notes. Do not worry about the content of the discussion. Take as many notes as possible. They will be very necessary to the discussion later.

37

An Assignment for Sharing: The "Ten-Most-Preferred" List*

Louis Thayer

Goals

    I. To encourage the participants to assess their reading habits and selections.

    II. To help the group members get to know each other better by discussing what they read or would like to read and the reasons for their selections.

Group Size

Small groups of six to eight people or a large group of twenty to twenty-five.

Time Required

Two group meetings—one for distribution of assignment and the second for group discussion. The discussion phase takes approximately twenty-five minutes for small groups, forty-five minutes for a large group.

Physical Setting

A large room with each group's chairs arranged in a circle.

Materials

    I. A copy of the "Ten-Most-Preferred" Assignment Sheet for each participant.

    II. Paper and pencils.

---

*From "An Assignment for Sharing: The 'Ten Most Preferred' List," by L. C. Thayer, *New Directions in Teaching*, 1974, 4(3), 39-41. Copyright © 1974 by Office of Experimental Studies, Bowling Green State University, Bowling Green, Ohio. Adapted and reprinted by permission.

Step-by-Step Process

I. At the first group meeting (or at the end of a regular meeting), the facilitator distributes copies of the "Ten-Most-Preferred" Assignment Sheet and explains the assignment. He asks the participants to come to the next session with their assignments.

II. At the second meeting, the participants form small groups of six to eight people. The participants distribute copies of their assignment to the other group members.

III. The facilitator asks the participants to discuss their reading lists and to give reasons for their selections. Particular attention can be given to the kinds of themes developed in each person's list (e.g., survival), or to the types of books (e.g., novels, biographies, science fiction).

IV. The facilitator distributes pencils and paper and asks the participants to make a list of books that they wish to read. Often good bibliographies are generated in this phase.

V. The facilitator suggests that the participants may want to loan books to other members or discuss their choices with people who have similar views or with those who have different views.

VI. The facilitator leads a group discussion on the book selections, the participants' reading habits, and setting new goals for reading.

Variations

The following statements offer several variations of the assignment.

1. Make a list of no more than ten people with whom you would share the rest of your life if for some unknown reason there could be no others. Try to explain your choice of each person on the list.

2. Make a list of no more than ten careers that you would like to have if for some unknown reason you learned about your future and discovered that you would change careers ten times in your lifetime. Try to give reasons for your selections and rank your choices according to your level of interest.

3. Make a list of no more than ten major achievements that you will accomplish (or would like to accomplish) in your lifetime if for some unknown reason you were able to predict accurately your future. Try to rank the achievements in order of importance to you and explain the meaning each holds for you.

4. Make a list of no more than ten principles by which you wish to live your life if for some unknown reason you were expected to present your principles for review before a committee on living. Try to justify the inclusion of each principle on your list and indicate how these principles would be reflected in your behavior.

5. Make a list of no more than ten people who have had a significant influence on your life style (values, attitudes, behaviors) if for some unknown reason you could choose no others. Try to describe each person briefly and note the characteristics you like and dislike.

6. Make a list of no more than ten life incidents, situations, or experiences that have had a significant impact on your goals for life and career direction. Try to give reasons for your choices and note the roles played by other people.

7. Make a list of no more than ten pieces of music (records, sheet music) that you would like to keep for life if for some unknown reason you could have no others. Try to give reasons for each selection.

8. Write a different assignment with your learning group in mind, for example,
   Make a list of no more than ten _____ that you would _____ if for some unknown reason you could have no others. Try to give reasons for each point on your list.

Notes

There are numerous other topics for consideration that can easily be adapted for any age level and for most classroom subjects. Topical themes may also focus on the past, present, or future with an emphasis on people, experiences, etc. Each classroom facilitator can develop his own topics. Here are additional topics for consideration.

1. Historical events;
2. Favorite friends, teachers, bosses;
3. Poems, novels, history books, authors;
4. Professors, counselors, helpers;
5. Values, life goals;
6. Worldly possessions, articles of value;
7. Places of residence, travel;
8. Meaningful successes.

Once the topical theme or a combination of stimulus statements is chosen, a method for sharing must be established—one-to-one, triads, small groups, large groups, or various combinations. If the facilitator wishes students to receive feedback on the ways in which they are perceived, he should include in his method an opportunity for each person to give and receive feedback from each person in his group. This process works well in small groups of six to eight people.

Reference

Peterson, S. *A catalog of the ways people grow.* New York: Ballantine, 1971.

"TEN-MOST-PREFERRED" ASSIGNMENT SHEET

In order to begin a sharing and self-assessment process, which I hope will be the tone of our group, consider for a moment all the books that you have ever read or would like to read. Please make a list of no more than *ten* books that you would keep if for some unknown reason you could have no others. Duplicate eight copies of your list. Also try to remember the reasons for your selections. Please try to give the complete reference for each book, as indicated by the following example:

Castaneda, Carlos. *The Teachings of Don Juan.* New York: Ballantine, 1969.

38

What's Your Thing?: Value Orientations

Ajit K. Das

Goals

   I. To increase the participants' awareness of fundamental values that influence their decision-making behavior.

   II. To encourage the awareness of similarities and differences between the participants' value orientations.

   III. To help the participants discover what persons, objects, and events they value intrinsically and how they would rank-order these values according to their significance in the participants' lives.

Group Size

Small groups of six to eight people.

Time Required

Approximately one hour.

Physical Setting

A carpeted room.

Materials

Chalkboard, chalk, paper, and pencils.

Step-by-Step Process

   I. The facilitator explains the concept of intrinsic value, differentiating it from the concept of instrumental value, and lists several examples of intrinsic values (health, happiness, beauty, knowledge, freedom, power, etc.) on the chalkboard.

II. He then distributes pencils and paper and asks each participant to make a composite list of the objects that have intrinsic value for him.

III. The facilitator asks the participants to rank-order these values according to their significance in their lives.

IV. He divides the large group into small groups of six to eight people each.

V. Each member of the subgroups is asked to share his list of intrinsic values with others in his group.

VI. The facilitator encourages the participants to share their feelings and reactions to the commonness and difference between their lists and the lists of others.

VII. The facilitator reassembles the large group to initiate a general discussion on the relationship between values and behavior in situations involving alternatives and decisions.

Variations

I. In the small groups, the group members can try to guess an individual's intrinsic values based on their knowledge of him. This guessing can be done several times before the sharing of the value lists. Accurate perceptions of other people's preferences can be checked.

II. The participants can be encouraged to conduct this values-clarification activity with a friend, a spouse, a boss, or a colleague to enhance communication and understanding.

III. Although this structured experience can be used with any group, it is likely to work best with a heterogeneous group with diverse value orientations.

39

Marcus Welby's Dilemma: A Values-Exploration Activity

Craig L. Dreilinger

Goals

I. To clarify one's value system regarding drug abuse and authority relationships.

II. To enhance the participants' communication skills, team relationships, and team functioning.

III. To study group processes that facilitate and block group decision making.

IV. To explore processes involving value confrontations, hidden agendas, and authority relationships.

Group Size

Six to twelve participants. Additional participants may be used as observers. Several groups may be directed simultaneously.

Time Required

Ninety minutes for part one; 120 minutes for part two.

Materials

I. Newsprint and a felt-tipped marker.

II. Paper and a pencil for each participant.

III. A copy of the What Would Marcus Welby Do? Sheet for each participant.

IV. A copy of the Marcus Welby's Dilemma Personal Preference Form for each participant.

V. A copy of the appropriate Marcus Welby's Dilemma Role-Briefing Sheet for each role player.

Step-by-Step Process

I. (Part One.) The facilitator introduces the goals of the activity and distributes pencils, copies of the What Would Marcus Welby Do? Sheet, and copies of the Marcus Welby's Dilemma Personal Preference Form.

II. He explains the instructions and allows the participants ten minutes to read the sheet and to fill out the form.

III. The facilitator asks each participant to announce how he ranked each character on the personal preference form. He instructs the participants to record the individual rankings on their personal preference form. Concurrently, he records the results on newsprint.

IV. The facilitator tells the group that its task is to reach a group consensus on the rank ordering. (Approximately one hour is allowed for this process.) The facilitator does not become involved in the group interactive process.

V. After the group has completed its task, the facilitator introduces a discussion on the interactive processes used to reach consensus and the differences in personal values regarding drug abuse and authority relationships. He also points out specific instances of effective communication skills.

VI. (Part Two.) The facilitator assigns a role from the Marcus Welby's Dilemma Role-Briefing Sheet to five group members. He also assigns a sixth role: the role of Jan from the What Would Marcus Welby Do? Sheet. The facilitator may assign additional roles from the sheet if the group is large. Additional participants may be asked to observe the role play and to take notes of the interaction.

VII. After all roles have been assigned, the facilitator gives the role players about ten minutes to study their roles. He informs the role players not to divulge the nature of their roles during the process, except to give their names and positions.

VIII. The facilitator describes the nature of the meeting to be held: Following her dismissal, Jan asks to appear before the Sopor Hospital Review Committee (SHRC) to appeal Dr. Henry's decision to fire her. The committee, composed of five members, usually operates by consensus; only three out of five votes are required to reach a decision. Jan is presenting her own case to the review committee. Mr. Dawson is the committee chairperson.

IX. The facilitator instructs the review committee to begin its hearing and to continue until a decision has been reached.

X. At the conclusion of the hearing, the facilitator reassembles the large group. The role players explain their roles and discuss the ways in which their hidden agendas were manifested.

XI. The facilitator and/or the observers provide feedback on the committee meeting and the decision-making process. The facilitator helps the participants examine the attitudes, exhibited behaviors, and values implicit in each role player's interactions, focusing on drug abuse and authority relationships.

Variations

I. If process observers are used, some of them may be assigned specific tasks, such as noting all value statements, instances of good communication skills, examples of helping behaviors, and observations of each individual in the group.

II. The first two steps of the activity may be completed as a homework assignment for the next group session.

III. The facilitator could alter the circumstances of the vignette or describe the conflict taking place in a different environmental setting.

IV. The activity could be divided into two sessions to provide sufficient time for process assessment.

V. The group can decide to pursue other topical areas that focus on values clarification.

VI. An elaborate observer's sheet could be prepared prior to the role play in order for the observers to watch for particular behaviors, values, attitudes, and group processes.

VII. The group may wish to invite several professional people to the role play to consider other values and attitudes that are often confronted.

VIII. The role players may be instructed to act on any new perceptions or behaviors learned from the discussions about group process in the first part of the activity.

IX. Homework assignments may be given in conjunction with the activities in Parts I and II. The participants may be asked to prepare a paper on values clarification, on values reaffirmed, or on values challenged by others. For some, a paper on the analysis of the total group process may be a good way in which to assess group behavior and each individual's own behavior in a group.

X. The role-briefing sheets can be altered to fit other institutional settings, such as the public secondary school or university counseling center.

WHAT WOULD MARCUS WELBY DO? SHEET

Dorothy calls Help Line, a local hotline/crisis intervention center, explaining in a quivering voice, "I took a tab of acid an hour ago and now I'm getting real scared. My hands and feet are getting numb. I think maybe I got some PCP by mistake. I'm afraid maybe I'm going to freak out."

Craig, a volunteer for Help Line and a paraprofessional counselor (B.A. in psychology, fourteen months experience as a crisis-intervention worker), drives over and picks up Dorothy. Craig explains that if she mistakingly took PCP it would help account for the symptoms she described. She is scared, but lucid. Together they decide to go to the hospital emergency department just to be safe—as long as Craig promises that Dorothy will not be forced to take any medication against her will. Craig readily agrees.

On arriving at the emergency department, Craig sees Jan, a registered nurse with whom he is friendly. Seeing lots of other people waiting and knowing that Dorothy is feeling "shaky," Craig asks Jan if she can let Dorothy stay in an empty, private room while she waits to see a doctor (which will probably take a full hour).

Jan agrees with Craig and asks Dr. Henry, a resident, for his permission to break regular procedure and to allow Craig and Dorothy to use the room. Dr. Henry is sympathetic, but says that they can use the room only if Dorothy promises to provide information to the police (as required by state law) and if she will agree to medication (probably an injection of phenothiazine) if he decides it is needed.

Jan says neither yes nor no, but quietly returns to Craig and Dorothy and lets them into the private room. Fifteen minutes later, although Dorothy is feeling better, Jan becomes increasingly afraid of the consequences of going behind Dr. Henry's back. She goes to Dr. Klein for advice, but he refuses to become involved. Finally she returns to Dr. Henry and agrees to his terms, but does not inform Craig or Dorothy of her action.

Eventually Dr. Henry sees Dorothy. He explains that she will have to give Jan certain information and prescribes Thorazine and overnight observation. Dorothy becomes terrified and screams. Craig rushes into the examining room, discovers what has happened, and refuses to allow the treatment. Angered, he says that he and Dorothy had not agreed to the conditions. Dr. Henry, realizing that Jan had acted on her own, terminates her on the spot.

MARCUS WELBY'S DILEMMA
PERSONAL PREFERENCE FORM

Instructions: In the first blank column of the chart below, rank-order the characters in the What Would Marcus Welby Do? Sheet with the numbers 1, 2, 3, 4, and 5: 1 for the character toward whose actions, values, and attitudes you feel closest, i.e., the character you respect the most; 5 for the least-respected character. Record the responses of the other members of your group in the remaining columns when instructed by the facilitator.

Characters	Your Preference	Group Members' Preference							
		1	2	3	4	5	6	7	8
Dorothy									
Craig									
Jan									
Dr. Henry									
Dr. Klein									

MARCUS WELBY'S DILEMMA ROLE-BRIEFING SHEET

Role 1

Marvin Meltzer, M.D. You are a psychiatrist, only recently affiliated with the hospital and the committee. You are anxious to be well liked by members of the hospital staff and eventually hope to move into an administrative position that would give you more prestige, power, and money.

Role 2

Mrs. Bogglot. You are fifty-two years old and head nurse in the emergency department of Sopor Hospital. Although you were not present the evening that the incident occurred, you know both Nurse Jan and Dr. Henry. You believe strongly that the emergency department is effective when run "tightly," i.e., you believe in a strict code of rules made to be followed closely.

Role 3

Mr. Dawson. You are forty-four years old, married but separated, the president of Sopor Hospital's board of directors, and the chairperson of the review committee. You have no advance opinion of this case, but you do find Nurse Jan attractive and for some time have contemplated asking her for a date.

Role 4

Miss Rupp. You are twenty-six years old, a clerk-receptionist at the hospital, and a representative of Hospital Union Local #406, a union for nonprofessional workers. You have believed for a long time that the hospital discriminates against lesser professionals, nonprofessionals, and women. You resent this and harbor ill feelings, but you have not as yet actively voiced your resentment.

Role 5

Jack Claims. You are twenty-eight years old, a local citizen, and a community representative for the review committee. You have thought for quite some time that Sopor Hospital is a cold, rigid, and uncomfortable place, although it provides very good services. You believe that if the hospital were run more loosely, it would be a friendlier place and one more likely utilized by the people.

40

Educational Planning Committee: Group Consensus Seeking

Carol A. Burden

Goals

I. To help the participants clarify the combination of skills, education, and experiences that are valued for educational planning committees.

II. To help the participants examine their reasons for selecting or rejecting certain educators for a committee.

III. To review the interactive processes in consensus seeking.

Group Size

Several groups of six to twelve participants each.

Time Required

Approximately one hour.

Physical Setting

A room large enough for several small groups to interact without disturbing each other.

Materials

I. Pencils and a copy of the Educational Planning Committee Candidates Sheet for each participant.

II. A tape recorder (optional).

Step-by-Step Process

I. The facilitator divides the participants into small groups of six to twelve persons and distributes pencils and the Educational Planning Committee Candidates Sheets. He goes over the instructions and answers any questions. At least two people in each group are designated to be observers of the group process and the related content. One observer is instructed to note the group's interactive processes for later feedback to the group. The other observer is asked to monitor the values and issues raised as the educational planning committee is selected.

II. Each participant is asked to choose six people from the list of ten candidates whom he would support for the committee positions. (Allow seven to ten minutes.)

III. The facilitator asks the group members to reach consensus on six candidates who should be selected for the committee positions. Each group will later be asked to present its six choices to the total group with supporting rationale for each selection. (A maximum of twenty minutes is suggested for this step.)

IV. After each group reaches consensus, the facilitator reconvenes the total group to present and compare the subgroups' selections and supporting rationale.

V. At this point, the facilitator asks the observers from each group to share their observations of their group's interactive processes and their lists of values and issues raised in selecting the final six people. The facilitator is careful to point out when participants make assumptions based on past experiences with certain "types" of educators, when they show prejudice in selections, etc.

VI. The facilitator continues the discussion to help clarify the effects of the participants' attitudes and values on the selection of the committee members.

Variations

I. The facilitator may wish to devise an observation sheet for each different type of observer.

II. After step III, the facilitator could ask the participants to write down their impressions of the values and issues raised, their role in the group decision-making process, and their perceptions of the overall interactive process. These lists could be compared with observers' notes in step V.

III. The format may be used for other situations by altering the descriptive statements. Other groups interested in educational planning would find this experience helpful in reviewing group process, educational values, and consensus seeking.

EDUCATIONAL PLANNING COMMITTEE CANDIDATES SHEET

A new educational planning committee is being established with your school district. The committee will have broad responsibilities for making recommendations to the school board for educational policy changes. The committee will be supported by the local teachers' association and will be quite powerful.

Your task is to select six people from the following list of ten who will serve on the educational planning committee.

Place a check mark (✔) next to the names of your choice. Write your reasons for selecting each person in the space provided.

_____ A 36-year-old female with a master's degree in elementary education. She has taught eight years in grades 3, 4, 5, and 6, runs a tight classroom, and is open to new ideas.
Reasons:

_____ A 26-year-old male art teacher with one year of teaching experience. He has creative ideas, works well with students in elementary school, and has added new interest in the community by showing works of artists and outstanding students.
Reasons:

_____ A 45-year-old black female with twenty years of teaching experience. She knows primary-school children best, but has taught at all levels. Children's literature is one of her specialties.
Reasons:

_____ A 27-year-old female teacher who has just completed her fifth year of teaching. She is an exciting and innovative teacher, well liked by students, who has strong opinions that continually challenge the school administration. She has been a strong supporter of the union movement in education.
Reasons:

_____ A 55-year-old male physical education specialist who has coached Little League baseball in the summer and has worked as a boy scout volunteer. He has taught for twelve years and was in the military prior to entering education.
Reasons:

_____ A 30-year-old male with eight years' teaching experience in science and math. He conducts summer nature excursions for children and adults and he is soon to complete his master's degree in science.
Reasons:

_____ A 38-year-old female reading specialist with a K-12 certificate. She is thoroughly knowledgeable of developmental reading skills and is extremely competent in the diagnosis and remediation of reading difficulties.
Reasons.

_____ A 25-year-old Oriental female drama teacher who plays the oboe in the local symphony. She also has had experience with the local dance group.
Reasons:

_____ A 33-year-old male psychologist who is very service oriented. He is readily approached by his colleagues and has had considerable success in working with students who have had emotional and academic problems.
Reasons:

_____ A 22-year-old female ex-Peace Corps participant with teaching credentials. She has just returned from Thailand, where she developed an outstanding community program that focused on the active participation of parents in the educational experiences of their children. She would like to begin her teaching career in the U.S. and is eager to develop an innovative program in the language arts and social studies area.
Reasons:

41

Public Attitudes Toward Education: Group Consensus Seeking

Kent D. Beeler

Goals

I. To alert the participants to the layman's overall attitudes regarding the major problems confronting public school education.

II. To allow the participants to assess and compare their individual, average individual, and group decision-making scores with other participants and groups.

III. To enable the participants to experience a group consensus-seeking activity and to share feelings about the decision-making process.

Group Size

Small groups of five to six participants.

Time Required

Approximately sixty minutes for the activity, with additional time for discussion.

Physical Setting

A room large enough for the groups to meet without interfering with each other.

Materials

I. Pencils.

II. A copy of the Public Attitudes Individual Worksheet for each participant.

III. A copy of the Public Attitudes Group Instructions Sheet for each participant.

IV. A copy of the Public Attitudes Group Worksheet for each group.

V. A copy of the Public Attitudes Directions-for-Scoring Sheet for each group recorder.

VI. A copy of the Public Attitudes Actual Ranking Sheet for each group recorder.

Step-by-Step Process

I. The facilitator divides the participants into small groups of five to six people and gives each individual a pencil and a copy of the Public Attitudes Individual Worksheet. He informs the participants that they are to rank the ten major problems in education under three levels of frequency. He explains that the participants are to work independently during this step.

II. After fifteen minutes, the facilitator announces that a group ranking is to be made. He distributes the Public Attitudes Group Instructions Sheets and reads the instructions and guidelines to be followed in reaching consensus.

III. The facilitator gives a Public Attitudes Group Worksheet to each group. Each group designates a recorder to keep track of the group's consensus ranking for each item on the worksheet. The groups are given thirty minutes to reach consensus on the ten problems. The participants are instructed not to change any answers on their individual worksheets as a result of the group discussion.

IV. The facilitator gives each group recorder a copy of the Public Attitudes Directions-for-Scoring Sheet and a copy of the Public Attitudes Actual Ranking Sheet. Each recorder directs the scoring process for his group.

V. The recorders report their average individual and group scores to the facilitator for comparison with the other groups.

VI. The facilitator leads a total-group discussion on the implications of the attitudes toward education, helps participants compare the education poll results with local school operations, and assists them in exploring ways in which they can influence public opinion.

VII. The facilitator focuses the discussion on the participants' experiences during the consensus-seeking activity. The participants should be encouraged to discuss their feelings, which can be related to other groups in which they participate. Goals for behavioral change can be discussed and set.

Variations

I. Any roster of similar items that can be conveniently or arbitrarily ranked or grouped under three or four levels can be adapted to this format.

II. Students of all ages can revise and adapt this format for individual group studies and research projects. Various topical themes besides education may be used.

Reference

Gallup, G. H. Seventh annual Gallup poll of public attitudes toward education. *Phi Delta Kappan*, 1975, 56(4), 227-241.

PUBLIC ATTITUDES INDIVIDUAL WORKSHEET

The Ford Foundation-Gallup education poll is a major source of information concerning the status and trend of opinions about significant school questions. The 1975 poll of the lay public's attitudes toward education provided ten major problems with which the public schools in their community must deal.

Instructions: Assume the role of the average lay citizen and adopt his attitude toward public school education. Rank the ten most frequently mentioned problems under three levels.

List of Problems
A. Use of drugs
B. Size of school/classes
C. Lack of proper financial support
D. Crime/vandalism/stealing
E. Integration/segregation/busing
F. Poor curriculum
G. Lack of proper facilities
H. Difficulty of getting "good" teachers
I. Pupils' lack of interest
J. Lack of discipline

First Level of Frequency

1. (   )
2. (   )
3. (   )

Second Level of Frequency

4. (   )
5. (   )
6. (   )

Third Level of Frequency

7. (   )
8. (   )
9. (   )
10. (   )

Individual Score (   )

PUBLIC ATTITUDES GROUP INSTRUCTIONS SHEET

Instructions: This is an exercise in group decision making. Your group is to employ the group consensus method in reaching its decision. This means that the placement of each of the ten major educational problems *must* be agreed upon by each group member before it becomes a part of the group decision. Consensus is not easily reached, and not every ranking will meet with everyone's *complete* approval. However, try, as a group, to make each ranking one with which *all* group members can at least *partially* agree. Here are some guidelines to follow in reaching consensus.

1. Avoid arguing endlessly for your own individual judgments. Approach the task on the basis of logic.
2. Avoid changing your mind if it is only to reach agreement and avoid conflict. Support only the solutions with which you are able to agree at least somewhat.
3. Avoid "conflict-reducing" techniques such as majority-rule voting, averaging, and trading in reaching your decision.

PUBLIC ATTITUDES GROUP WORKSHEET

List of Problems

- A. Use of drugs
- B. Size of school/classes
- C. Lack of proper financial support
- D. Crime/vandalism/stealing
- E. Integration/segregation/busing
- F. Poor curriculum
- G. Lack of proper facilities
- H. Difficulty of getting "good" teachers
- I. Pupils' lack of interest
- J. Lack of discipline

First Level of Frequency

1. (   )
2. (   )
3. (   )

Second Level of Frequency

4. (   )
5. (   )
6. (   )

Third Level of Frequency

7. (   )
8. (   )
9. (   )
10. (   )

Group Score (   )

Average Individual Score (   )

PUBLIC ATTITUDES DIRECTIONS-FOR-SCORING SHEET

As group recorder you are responsible for directing the scoring of your group.

1. Read the data from the Public Attitudes Actual Ranking Sheet and ask the participants to total the number of attitudes placed under the correct level of frequency.* Ask the group members to report their individual scores to you.

2. Total the individual scores and divide by the number of participants to arrive at an average individual score.

3. Score the group worksheet and place both the group score and the average individual score on it.

Ratings:

10-8   Excellent

7-5   Good

4-3   Average

2-1   Fair

---

*Note that the goal of the exercise was to rank under three levels the ten most frequently mentioned problems in public education. It is not necessary to have placed each problem in the exact order in which it appears in the actual rankings, only to have placed a problem in the correct level of frequency.

PUBLIC ATTITUDES ACTUAL RANKING SHEET

First Level of Frequency

1. J—Lack of discipline
2. E—Integration/segregation/busing
3. C—Lack of proper financial support

Second Level of Frequency

4. H—Difficulty of getting "good" teachers
5. B—Size of school/classes
6. A—Use of drugs

Third Level of Frequency

7. F—Poor curriculum
8. D—Crime/vandalism/stealing
9. G—Lack of proper facilities
10. I—Pupils' lack of interest

42

The September-to-December Runaround Blues: A Simulation

Margaret J. Barr and Geoffrey E. Grant

Goals

I. To assist students in identifying the many referral and service agencies located on a college campus.

II. To provide students with an opportunity to recognize their own adjustment or survival needs.

Group Size

The simulation requires one staff member per "office" or "agency" represented in the simulation. It also requires one game manager. When the simulation phase is complete, these same staff personnel become co-leaders for the discussion groups.

The number of participants can vary according to the size of the room or the number of "offices" represented. A minimum of fifty participants permits the build-up of lines at the simulation. Given the proper facilities and staff, as many as 150 to 200 students can participate at one time.

Time Required

Approximately ninety minutes. The game is designed in two parts: the actual simulation (thirty minutes), and the discussion phase (forty-five minutes to one hour).

Physical Setting

A large room, at least 30' by 50', e.g., a small gym or a cafeteria, and a waiting room.

Prior to the simulation, the game manager sets up the "offices" by placing tables around the periphery of the room, with sufficient chairs near them so that the students can sit while waiting for assistance. The "offices" are identified only by a small sign at the front of the respective tables. A "map" that locates the "offices" or "agencies" within the room should be posted behind the General Information Desk.

Materials

I. One desk and three or four chairs per staff "office."

II. A list of ten to fifteen tasks for each student, prepared in advance by the game manager. (There should be some variety of lists with some different tasks to create flexibility.)

III. A microphone and a "map" of offices.

IV. A copy of the Instructions for Game Personnel for each staff member.

V. A copy of the Instructions for Students for each student.

VI. A time clock.

VII. Small signs indicating the various campus offices: a college professor's office, the Financial Aids Office, the Health Center, the Campus Police, the Housing Office, the Dean of Students' Office, the Reading and Study Skills Laboratory, the Student Union, the Counseling Center, the General Information and Referral Service, the Registrar, the Admissions Office, the Career Choice Information Center, the Academic Dean's Office, and Passionate Peggy's Bar. Although this simulation focuses on the college campus, the game manager can prepare his own list of "offices" to be representative of a university or an institution.

Step-by-Step Process

I. Prior to the simulation, the game manager and the staff members participate in a staff training session regarding their roles and the game's objectives. The game manager assigns one staff member to each office and distributes copies of the Instructions for Game Personnel. Copies of the student tasks that are associated with each "office" are supplied to assist the game personnel, in addition to any other materials or forms that they may need. (Allow ten minutes for the game personnel to read the sheets.)

II. When the students are ready to begin the simulation, the game manager explains the game and informs them about the list of tasks that they are to complete before the "semester" time clock runs out. He explains that the students may also be faced with emergency situations that are to be resolved during the simulation period. They do not receive any specific directions about the order or importance of the tasks on their lists. The game manager explains that after the students have completed their lists of tasks, they may help other students.

III. As the students enter the room in which the simulation is staged, the game manager hands out a copy of the Instructions for Students and a list of tasks to each student. He should also indicate where the "map" of offices and the General Information and Referral Service are located.

IV. During the simulation, the game manager periodically carries out certain duties, such as closing "offices" for vacation periods (one to two minutes), informing game personnel of their phone calls, creating emergencies, etc.

V. At the end of the thirty-minute simulation, the game manager divides the students into discussion groups, which are led by staff members who have manned the "offices." (The discussion leaders may wish to conduct a short getting-acquainted activity prior to the group discussion.) The purpose of the discussion is to examine the goals and outcomes of the simulation, focusing on what "hassles" the students encountered, what good experiences they had, and which offices were particularly helpful for certain kinds of information. Questions such as the following may be asked: How did the students cope with uncooperative staff members? Were other students helpful to them? What frustrations were experienced? The discussion groups should take advantage of all the situational information that has occurred. These discussions should exhaust all questions and anxieties that have arisen. If this simulation is part of a larger program, it may be possible to reference other program components that elaborate on this experience or information.

Variations

I. This activity can also help current staff professionals, who take on the role of students for the referral game, to empathize with students' frustrations and their inability to cope in a foreign environment. If a sufficient number of new staff (primarily paraprofessionals like graduate and undergraduate residence-hall staff) need orientation to the various services and agencies, the referral game can likewise provide a meaningful experience.

II. The rudiments of this game can be rather easily adapted to other clientele and settings that involve the consistent exchange of agency services and referral procedures.

III. Ideally, the game manager may be able to involve actual staff from the various university campus offices in designing the lists of tasks for the students to complete, in preparing the materials to be used by each office, in developing various emergencies to be used during the game, in participating in the actual simulation, and in leading group discussions after the simulation.

Notes

For many people, especially new students, the college or university is a large, complex institution. Students are faced with many choices and decisions as they begin their college careers. In such an institution, there are many referral agencies to assist students in resolving problems. However, oftentimes front-line staff may not be as responsive to individual students as students would like. Offices on campus may not be easily identifiable; they may move frequently. Signs on buildings often confuse students as to the actual function carried out within the building. Offices may be crowded, with long lines of students waiting to see a few staff members who have little time to spend with each student. This type of activity can help students become more informed about the agencies available to them.

INSTRUCTIONS FOR GAME PERSONNEL

Name of Office_____

You are to act as a representative of the office assigned to you. You should know what kinds of services are provided on the campus and why a student can legitimately come to see you. If you have any questions, see the game manager.

When a student comes to your desk to complete his assignment, sign his task sheet and send him on if you feel he has performed to your satisfaction. You may respond in a variety of ways, *but do not always be your usual helpful self.* Reflect on some of the experiences that students sometimes encounter from staff members on the campus. *Do not be consistent with all participants as the "semester" progresses.* You can change and react in different ways.

The following circumstances may help you choose several moods to adopt when working with the students.

1. The phone is ringing and you have a report due at 12 o'clock. It is now 11:45 a.m. and another student arrives.
2. You just received a merit raise and feel great.
3. Your sister is expecting a baby at any minute and you feel very nervous.
4. You know everything there is to know about the university—no one can tell you anything more.
5. You feel just great today and nothing can bother you.
6. You hate all those long-haired hippies, but you would do anything for those "nice" boys and girls.
7. You like students and want to help them.
8. You have been working at the university for twenty-seven years and are totally apathetic about student needs.
9. You have a new baby in the family that kept you awake last night and you are half asleep.

Use your judgment in how to approach each "student" based on these general guidelines. Do not unnecessarily hassle students, but also make them aware that they may receive erroneous information from campus offices and that they need to double-check to make sure that they are not misinformed. During the simulation, you should be aware of any announcements being made. You may be called, for instance, to an emergency phone call. The semester will proceed for approximately thirty minutes.

INSTRUCTIONS FOR STUDENTS

The tasks that have been assigned to you must be accomplished during a thirty-minute time period, which constitutes one semester. You may accomplish your tasks in any order that you desire. If you are confused about where to begin, the staff member at the General Information and Referral Service can assist you in finding the proper referral services on campus. You will also note that there is a "map" of offices posted behind the General Information Desk.

The most reliable source of information is the General Information and Referral Service office. You may also work with other students who are accomplishing some of the same tasks. Be aware, however, that misinformation regarding where to go for certain problems may be circulated by others. In order to assure that you have completed your tasks, you must have the agency or office representative sign your task sheet or refer you somewhere else for assistance in order to complete the task. Please listen for general directions, including times of office closings, emergencies, and so forth that will be announced periodically by microphone during the simulation. After you have completed all of your tasks, you should report to the Dean of Students' Office.

Now proceed to the "offices" to accomplish your tasks.

43

Future School:
A Simulation*

Charles M. Plummer

Goals

   I. To provide an opportunity for the participants to challenge or reaffirm some of their values toward and beliefs and assumptions about education.

  II. To explore how innovative procedures could be adopted in the participants' real or anticipated schools.

Group Size

An unlimited number of groups of four to six people.

Time Required

Approximately forty-five minutes.

Physical Setting

A large room or area in which the groups can interact without distracting each other.

Materials

   I. A copy of the Future School Introduction to Players Sheet.

  II. A copy of the Future School Rules and Procedures Sheet for each participant.

 III. A copy of the Future School Playing Procedures Sheet for each participant.

 IV. A Future School Game Board for each group.

---

*From Chronologic, 2309 North Headley Road, Bloomington, Indiana 47401. Copyright © 1976 by Charles M. Plummer. Adapted and reprinted by permission.

V. A packet of Event Cards, Knowledge Cards, and Free Draw Cards for each group. (See Instructions for Preparing Game Cards.)

VI. Board markers (coins or miscellaneous small objects).

VII. One die or a pair of dice for each group.

VIII. A clock or watch with a second hand for each group.

Step-by-Step Process

I. The facilitator introduces the game and divides the participants into small groups of four to six persons each.

II. He reads the directions on the Future School Introduction to Players Sheet and answers any questions.

III. Each participant receives a copy of the Future School Rules and Procedures Sheet and the Future School Playing Procedures Sheet. The facilitator responds to any questions and clarifies the game procedures.

IV. The facilitator gives each group a set of game materials—game board, event cards, knowledge cards, free draw cards, board markers, dice, and a clock—for the corresponding number of players in the group.

V. He establishes the playing time (or suggests how many players in each group must complete the game).

VI. The game begins.

VII. At the completion of the Future School game, the facilitator conducts a general discussion on the group dynamics and requests each group to assess different aspects of the game experience. Participants are encouraged to share which of their values, beliefs, and assumptions about education were challenged or reaffirmed.

Variations

I. The facilitator may wish to add another step to the process by asking the participants to focus on goals for behavioral change or for further study.

II. The game may be played a second time by altering the composition of the small groups.

III. Although designed primarily for classroom teachers, the Future School game can be used with most populations who are interested in schools—students, student-teachers, parents, administrators, school-board members, legislators, citizens groups such as parent-teacher associations, and others.

Notes

It has proven effective for the participants to follow the game by reading the introduction to Postman and Weingartner's (1969) proposals (chapter 8) and Rogers' (1969) implicit assumptions (chapter 8).

References

Greer, M., & Rubinstein, B. *Will the real teacher please stand up? A primer on humanistic education.* Pacific Palisades, Calif.: Goodyear, 1972.

Plummer, C. M. Social influence through simulation: Changing attitudes with the school game. *Viewpoints* (Bulletin of the School of Education). Bloomington: Indiana University, November 1973, 49(6), 39-47.

Plummer, C. M. *Social influence through simulation: Changing attitudes with the school game.* Paper presented at the American Educational Research Association Convention, Chicago, Illinois, April 1974.

Postman, N., & Weingartner, C. *Teaching as a subversive activity.* New York: Delacorte Press, 1969.

Rogers, C. R. *Freedom to learn.* Columbus, Ohio: Charles E. Merrill, 1969.

FUTURE SCHOOL INTRODUCTION TO PLAYERS SHEET

The Future School game is designed for the in-service and pre-service training of teachers. The obvious goal is to be the first person to land on the winning space (#46–"School's Out"). The general locale for the game is assumed to be a teacher's lounge, with players cast in the roles of teachers. Players take turns rolling the dice to see who can be the first person to get out of school. Success is dependent not only on the throw of the dice, but upon skill in (a) guessing which assumptions students are likely to agree with, and (b) persuading others that certain specific innovative recommendations (supposedly from the school suggestion box) should be implemented immediately. Please note: anyone could have made the suggestion, including students, teachers, the principal, parents, taxpayers, a professor, a school-board member, the janitor, etc.

FUTURE SCHOOL RULES AND PROCEDURES SHEET

Objective: The objective of the game is to win by being the first person to get out of school.

Rules:

1. On the first throw, whoever rolls the highest number goes first, the next highest roll goes second, etc.

2. Use coins or similar small objects to mark your position on the game board.

3. Move ahead on the game board the number of spaces shown on the dice.

4. When you land on a space with instructions printed on it, follow those instructions faithfully, just as you do in real "school."

5. There are four kinds of spaces on the game board: Blank Spaces, Event Draw, Knowledge Draw, and Free Draw. If you land on a blank space, relax and wait for your next turn. If you land on the other spaces, draw a card and follow the directions.

    Event Card—Follow the instructions printed on the card. You may be told to move to another place on the board, move ahead, lose a turn, be quiet for one turn, etc.

    Knowledge Card—Indicate to the other players whether or not you agree or disagree with the statement printed on the card. Turn the card over to check your answer. If your answer is correct, you get to move ahead.

    Free Draw Card—Imagine that you are a teacher at a faculty meeting. Your task is to convince as many other teachers as possible that the proposals printed on the card are practical and should be implemented immediately in your school, even if you disagree with them! Since all the proposals were taken from the school "suggestion box," you become the "spokesman" for the anonymous suggestion writer.

    You have one minute to persuade the other players in your group to vote to implement the proposal on the card. Players are to vote only on the basis of the arguments you present. Only the other players may vote; your vote does not count. Move ahead the same number of spaces as the votes you win.

6. A round is over as soon as one player gets to space #46—"School's Out." *Note:* if the facilitator has allotted a time limit or instructed that more than one player should complete the game, continue to play.

7. Return the game materials to the facilitator when the time has expired or when the designated number of players have completed the game.

FUTURE SCHOOL PLAYING PROCEDURES SHEET*

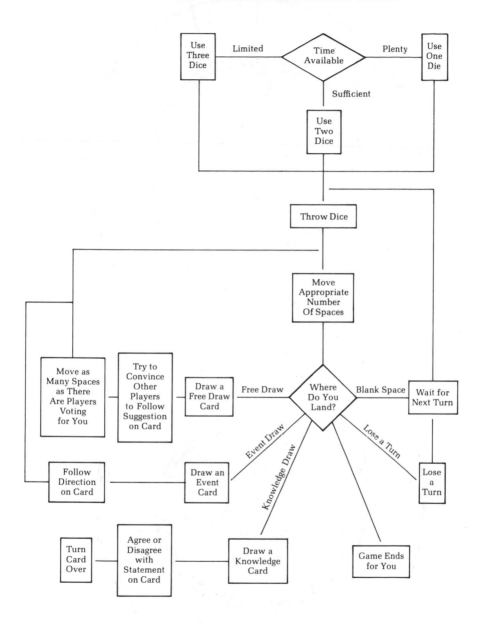

---

*Copyright © by Charles M. Plummer, 1976. Used with permission.

FUTURE SCHOOL GAME*

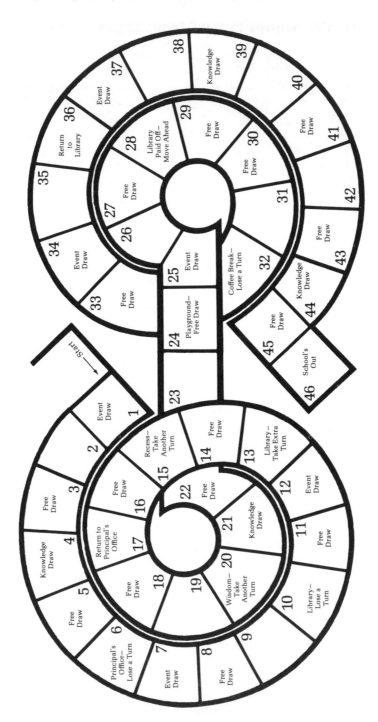

*The Future School Game is commercially available from Chronologic, 2309 North Headley Road, Bloomington, Indiana 47401. The cost is $5.00 per game.

INSTRUCTIONS FOR PREPARING GAME CARDS*

Directions: Write or type the messages for the game cards on unlined 3″ x 5″ index cards, using different colors for each type of draw card. Each Event Card has an instruction on one side of the card, e.g., "perfect attendance, move ahead five spaces." Each Knowledge Card has an assumption on one side of the card with which the card holder must agree or disagree; the other side has a message, e.g., "if you disagreed, move ahead one space." Each Free Draw Card has a proposal on one side, e.g., "require all teachers to take a one-year sabbatical every five years in a field other than education"; the obverse side of the card explains that the card holder has one minute to persuade others in his group to vote on the proposal.

EVENT CARDS

Event cards have a message only on one side.

Messages:

Sharpen your pencil.
Go ahead one space.

Lead the Pledge of Allegiance.
Advance one space.

Late for school.
Lose a turn.

Go to the library.

Teacher's pet.
Advance three spaces.

Be quiet for one turn.

Suspended for fighting.
Lose two turns.

Go to the principal's office.

You have a stomach ache. Go to the nurse's office (located two spaces behind where you are).

Fold your hands for one turn.

Gold star. Take another card.

Go to the auditorium (located one space ahead).

You have a pass to go to the bathroom. (There is no bathroom—you wet your pants. Lose one turn.)

Water the plants. Go ahead two spaces.

A smile from the teacher. Take another turn.

Busy work assignment. Stay where you are.

Suspended for smoking. Lose two turns.

Feed the fish. Go ahead one space.

Take a field trip. Move ahead three spaces.

Perfect attendance. Move ahead five spaces.

---

*The actual contents for the draw cards are based on three sources. The general outline for the game board and event cards is based on Greer and Rubinstein's *Will The Real Teacher Please Stand Up?* (1972). Knowledge cards are based on assumptions challenged by Carl Rogers in his book, *Freedom to Learn* (1969). Free draw cards involve provocative and controversial ideas taken from Postman and Weingartner's *Teaching as a Subversive Activity* (1969).

KNOWLEDGE CARDS

Front of Card *Assumptions:*	**Back of Card** *Messages:*
Paper-and-pencil tests can and should be used to predict long-term life success.	If you disagreed, move ahead two spaces.
The child is not an empty vessel.	If you agreed, move ahead two spaces.
Everything worth knowing is already known.	If you disagreed, move ahead two spaces.
The structure of the temple of knowledge is more than a carefully laid pile of stone.	If you agreed, move ahead two spaces.
The student learns what the teacher teaches.	If you disagreed, move ahead two spaces.
To achieve the highest levels of professional competence, those who will not profit from instruction should not be permitted to continue their education as far as *they* want to go.	If you disagreed, move ahead two spaces.
There is no learning without suffering.	If you disagreed, move ahead three spaces.
Student behavior is totally determined by external environmental manipulation.	If you disagreed, move ahead two spaces.
When a student flunks out of school, it is the student's fault, not the school's.	If you disagreed, move ahead two spaces.
Do not confuse the symbol for that which it represents, because what is measured is not always what is known. After all, the map is not the territory.	If you agreed, move ahead two spaces.
Active involvement is the key to creative learning.	If you agreed, move ahead three spaces.
Science is more than method.	If you disagreed, move ahead two spaces.

FREE DRAW CARDS

Front of Card *Proposals:*	Back of Each Card
All teachers must prove that they have been loved by at least one other human being other than their relatives *before* being allowed in a classroom that has real human beings.	You have *one minute* to persuade others in your group to vote to implement this proposal. Move ahead the same number of spaces as the votes you win.
Make all courses optional.	Repeat from above.
Measure teacher success in terms of student attainment of pre-specified behaviors.	Repeat.
Base teachers' salaries on demonstrated student interest.	Repeat.
Require all teachers to teach outside their subject-matter area.	Repeat.
Require that *every* question be treated as having more than one right answer in our school.	Repeat.
If the teacher already knows the answer, he should not ask students the question.	Repeat.
Teachers should measure all their success by observable student behaviors. *Example:* If the student did not learn it, in no way was it taught.	Repeat.
Teachers should be required to take a one-year sabbatical every five years to work in a field other than education (a mini-sabbatical for four months every two years is an acceptable alternative).	Repeat.

Front of Card	**Back of Each Card**
Prohibit the use of the following "educational jargon" words: "according to regulations," "because it's never been done before," or "yes, but not here," "red tape makes it impossible," or "there is no learning without suffering."	You have *one minute* to persuade others in your group to vote to implement this proposal. Move ahead the same number of spaces as the votes you win.
Lessons should be problem oriented.	Repeat from above.
Teach without using textbooks. Any other printed or nonprinted materials are acceptable.	Repeat.
Conduct all evaluations by means other than paper-and-pencil testing and grading.	Repeat.
Let students test teachers.	Repeat.
Make it illegal to "label" any student as "gifted" or "retarded," or any other stereo-typed category that distorts and oversimplifies the rich diversity and complexity of his unique human personality and potential.	Repeat.
Evaluate without any tests or grades.	Repeat.
Teachers should not be able to set standards of performance for a class without including the students' recommendations.	Repeat.
Teachers will be required to spend more time listening than talking in classes.	Repeat.
Recycle all graffiti from the bathroom to the hallway.	Repeat.

Front of Card	**Back of Each Card**
Let the teacher who "knows it all" write a book about it. Let only those who are interested buy the book. Classroom subject-matter talk will now be *student initiated.*	You have *one minute* to persuade others in your group to vote to implement this proposal. Move ahead the same number of spaces as the votes you win.
Prohibit corporal punishment in schools and other forms cruel and unusual, whether they be teacher to student, student to teacher, student to student, or teacher to teacher.	Repeat from above.
Let the students judge the "merit" of ideas without teacher domination.	Repeat.
Reassign all teachers to classrooms with students at least four years younger or older than those they now teach.	Repeat.
Publish student evaluations of teachers and give one copy of the ratings to every student.	Repeat.
Every teacher should be required to receive an annual "psychological" checkup and be certified "stable enough to facilitate human learning."	Repeat.
Substitute "behavioral objectives" for the "disciplines" or "content areas."	Repeat.
After the students speak, the teachers should not summarize what they have already said.	Repeat.
Let *learners* control all teaching for one semester.	Repeat.

Front of Card	Back of Each Card
Have teachers change roles with administrators, curriculum developers, teacher trainees, and their own students for at least one day each year.	You have *one minute* to persuade others in your group to vote to implement this proposal. Move ahead the same number of spaces as the votes you win.
Equalize educational opportunity.	Repeat from above.
Keep schools open for twelve months a year.	Repeat.
Individualize and personalize all instruction.	Repeat.
Let students go to any school they want to attend—and provide free transportation to them.	Repeat.
Let the lesson flow from the students' direct experiences and not from the teachers' experiences.	Repeat.
Keep schools open for twenty-four hours a day.	Repeat.
Require teachers to change schools every year.	Repeat.
Rescind compulsory schooling.	Repeat.
Make learning a life-long process.	Repeat.
Integrate athletic programs so that there are *no* single-sex teams.	Repeat.
Do not require all students to learn how to read in order to graduate from high school.	Repeat.

Front of Card	Back of Each Card
Teach alternative knowledge of and encourage experimentation with life styles, political philosophies, family forms, community and urban organization, social systems, cultures, technologies, and models for world order.	You have *one minute* to persuade others in your group to vote to implement this proposal. Move ahead the same number of spaces as the votes you win.
Initiate comprehensive and formalized sex education programs beginning in kindergarten.	Repeat from above.
Do away with "tenure" for teachers and college professors.	Repeat.
Make financial support of female athletic programs equal to male athletic programs.	Repeat.
Use the total community as an educational resource.	Repeat.
Forbid any form of "tracking" or "grouping" by ability levels.	Repeat.

44

Creativity Test: Intergroup Competition

Martin H. Crowe

Goal

To foster positive attitudes toward participatory, cooperative learning by defining components of creativity in a personally meaningful fashion.

Group Size

Any learning group.

Time Required

Forty to fifty minutes for a class of thirty-five people.

Physical Setting

Any classroom or comfortable setting in which the participants regularly meet.

Materials

    I. Paper and pencils.

   II. Desks or lapboards.

 III. An unusual object; for example, a poultry-juice baster, which is an unusual object composed of two parts—a rubber squeeze bulb and a long plastic tube.

Step-by-Step Process

    I. The facilitator distributes paper and pencils and presents the unusual object to the group with the following statement:

> "This object has several common uses, but I would like everyone to list as many uses for it as possible, no matter how unusual. [The facilitator takes the object apart.] These uses can

include just one part of it or both parts, assembled or disassembled. Take about five minutes to write down your responses."

II. After five minutes, the facilitator states that the participants' lists will be used to demonstrate some components of creativity. Each person reads his list to the group. As a group, the participants assess creativity "scores" for each person based on four components: number of uses, originality, flexibility, and elaboration. The process of scoring all these components as a group evokes strong feelings, particularly when the group decides if given responses are identical or different to determine the originality score.

   1. *Numerical Score*—The number of different uses listed for the unusual object.

   2. *Originality Score*—As each participant reads his list to the learning group, everyone checks off responses common to one or more of the other lists. The number of unique responses left is the originality score.

   3. *Flexibility Score*—The number of different categories covered in the list. Categories for the task might include (a) game uses, (b) functional uses, (c) writing-drawing uses, and (d) decorative uses.

   4. *Elaboration Score*—Each elaboration beyond the basic idea (one point for each).

III. The participants discuss their highest score and relate it to practical aspects of everyday life, e.g., are they truly creative in that (component) way? They also brainstorm for other components of creativity.

IV. The facilitator illustrates how the same processes are used for standardized creativity tests.

V. The facilitator asks the participants to cite, orally or in writing, examples of how they could utilize this activity to emphasize creativity in another learning setting.

Variations

I. This activity can be used with elementary school, secondary school, and college students. It can be used with small competitive groups as a cooperative learning activity that culminates in leap-frog brainstorming and discovering other uses for the object or the process.

II. The activity may be conducted several times by altering the unusual object. Participants can compare their scores each successive time.

III. Steps IV and V can be substituted with new steps that emphasize the development and training of creative potential.

IV. The facilitator may wish to assign a further review of a person's creativity and how it is manifested.

V. This activity can be fun at parties if the unusual objects are "unusual" enough.

Reference

Treffinger, D. J., & Gowan, J. C. An up-dated representative list of methods and educational programs for stimulating creativity. *The Journal of Creative Behavior,* 1971, 5(2), 127-139.

45

Look What They've Done to My Brain, Ma: An Exercise in Creativity and Self-Concept

Richard G. Nelson and James A. Gold

Goals

I. To illustrate the relationship between self-concept and creativity.

II. To enable the participants to experience the same feelings of anxiety as school pupils when they are ordered to be creative on demand.

III. To encourage the participants to focus on how they feel about their creative power and to realize that their peers have similar feelings.

Group Size

Fifteen to twenty people. Two groups may be conducted simultaneously or one group could act as observers.

Time Required

Fifty minutes.

Physical Setting

A classroom or conference room with easily moveable desks.

Materials

I. A pencil or pen, a blank sheet of unlined, 8½" x 11" paper, and two 3" x 5" index cards for each participant.

II. Chalkboard and chalk or newsprint and a felt-tipped marker.

Step-by-Step Process

I. The participants are asked to arrange the desks in a circle or to be seated around a large table. The facilitator announces to the group that this is an experiential activity in creativity. (The facilitator does *not* state the goals at the beginning of the activity because his expectations may inhibit the group's self-discovery.)

II. The facilitator distributes the paper, pencils, and index cards and asks the participants to draw a line about two inches to the right of the narrow side of the paper, as shown below:

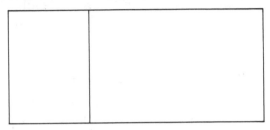

The space to the left of the line is for marginal notes. The large space to the right is for the person's "creation."

III. The facilitator tells the participants that they will have ten minutes to be creative. He may wish to comment that teachers often ask students to be creative on demand in composition, art, poetry, and other classes.

IV. Before the participants begin the assignment, the facilitator asks each person to write on the left side of the paper an adjective that describes how he feels about the activity.

V. The participants begin the activity. Anything is allowed—writing, paper folding, drawing, etc.

VI. After about five minutes into the creative assignment, the facilitator asks each person to write another adjective describing his present feelings. When each person has finished his paper, he is instructed to write down a third adjective describing his feelings.

VII. When the participants have completed their "creations" and their descriptive adjectives, the facilitator asks them to rate their own creations on a ten-point scale (ten is high), to place the score on one of the index cards, and to pass the card to him (anonymously).

VIII. The participants are asked to circulate their creations clockwise until they regain their own. Everyone should see each creation. Concurrently, the instructor computes the mean score for the group using the index cards.

IX. The facilitator asks the group to write on the other index card what they believe to be the average creative ability score of the group (ten is high). The cards are collected and a new mean is computed.

X. The group discusses the reasons for obtaining the two scores and what their meaning might represent. After some discussion, the facilitator writes the actual scores on chalkboard or on newsprint.

XI. Invariably, the self-judgment mean will be lower than the other-judgment mean. The facilitator continues the discussion, focusing on several points:
   1. The relationship between self-concept and creativity.
   2. Personal views of creative potential.
   3. Teachers as judges of creativity.
   4. Participant feelings/anxiety aroused by demanding creativity.
   5. Cultural demands and judgments on being creative.

Variations

I. To add another dimension, the facilitator may set himself up as a judge and compute the mean score on each creation. The facilitator would tell the participants early in the session that he would be a "judge."

II. The facilitator may wish to prepare a mini-lecture on the theory concerning self-concept and creativity for use in step X.

III. A logical follow-up training session may focus on fostering creativity and self-concepts in people.

IV. This activity may be used in various situations at different age levels where a person's self-concept, feelings, and other-judgments may affect creative potential and work satisfaction.

46

Image Recall: Your Thoughts and Feelings on Tests and Test Results

Louis Thayer

Goals

 I. To help the participants examine the development of their attitudes and perceptions of classroom and/or standardized tests and test results.

 II. To explore the participants' present feelings, thoughts, and opinions about the value of standardized tests and test results.

 III. To help the participants have more empathy for those who are required to take tests.

Group Size

Twenty to thirty participants.

Materials

Paper and pencils (optional).

Time Required

Approximately one hour.

Physical Setting

A room in which the participants can sit or lie down comfortably without touching one another.

Step-by-Step Process

 I. The facilitator suggests that the participants find a comfortable area in the room where they can be alone with their thoughts and feelings.

 II. The facilitator asks the participants to close their eyes and to become as physically relaxed as possible.

III. The participants are asked to join the facilitator in a short trip into their past. The facilitator tells them that they will be asked to recall previous testing situations in which they were involved. But first, they must become relaxed so they can "see" better during the trip.

IV. The facilitator instructs the participants to tighten their body muscles and to hold this tense position for several seconds before relaxing. The participants repeat this procedure three or four times. They are instructed to breathe deeply several times. The facilitator suggests that they let the relaxation flow over their bodies.

V. The facilitator reads the following stimulus statement in a very calm, soothing voice. During the image recall, he pauses at appropriate points for approximately twenty seconds.

"Try to form an image (picture) in your mind about the first testing situation in which you participated, the first time you ever remember taking a test ... [Pause] Now try to remember and picture the first time you ever took an IQ test. What was it like? How did you feel after the test? ... [Pause] Think about your elementary school years. Do you remember taking any achievement tests? How did they make you feel? Did you wonder what your teachers and parents would think of you and your scores? [Pause] Try to picture what the standardized tests were like in junior high school. Did anyone talk with you about the results? Did some teachers expect more of you or less of you as a result of the tests? Were you smart, according to the teachers? [Pause] Did your parents ever go to conferences on your test results? If so, what were the effects on you? [Pause] Now think about your high school days. What were the standardized tests like then? How did you feel when you took the tests? Did someone, perhaps a counselor or a teacher, interpret the results for you? [Pause] Remember your last year in high school. Did you take tests for entrance into college? Did anyone encourage or discourage your future plans because of any standardized test scores? Were you worried about college because of your test scores? Did your scores present a true picture of your aptitude and achievements? Did anyone really know your abilities and desires for the future? If so, who was that person? [Pause] Did you know your IQ then (or now)? Did it help you by knowing it? [Pause] Now remember your encounter with tests after you left high school. What were they like—college tests, placement tests, standardized tests, entrance tests, civil service tests, army tests, and others? How did they help or hinder you? [Pause] Have you ever been told that your scores were not quite high enough for a job or a profession? How did you feel? Do you have certain thoughts, feelings, and attitudes about tests because of your experiences? What are they? [Pause] Remember the start of this school year? The principal told you what standardized tests had to be administered. Did you have any empathy for the students or any thoughts about giving the tests? What were they? Would you expect certain levels of work from certain students? Will you label those in your class? [Pause] Remember how you felt about attending this session today. What were your thoughts? Did you think it would be worthwhile? Could it change your attitudes or use of test results? Remember walking into the room and seeing me? Did you think it would be interesting or helpful? What was going on inside you? [Pause] Remember when I asked you to get comfortable? What reactions did you have? Try to focus on your responses as we took the short trip. Think back over the thoughts you had about testing. Did it help you recall your thoughts and feelings about tests? How have your experiences influenced your attitudes and behaviors with tests? [Pause] Pay attention to all that is going on within your body and your mind. Pay particular attention now to your thoughts. Think of some precise words that could describe your attitudes about tests . . . your uses of test results . . . the expectations you set for students . . . the changes you wish to make. [Pause] Now stretch your arms and legs, move your head around, and open your eyes."

VI. After the participants have emerged from the image recall, the facilitator asks the participants to form small groups for discussion purposes. He encourages them to relate some of their testing experiences, noting their positive and negative feelings. The facilitator also suggests that each group select a recorder to list the various helpful and hindering effects experienced by group participants in taking tests.

VII. After sufficient time is allowed for the participants to relate their past experiences, the facilitator asks them to discuss their present attitudes and how these are reflected in behavior in a work setting. The question can be posed: "How much will you rely on standardized test results for yourselves or for those with whom you work or teach?"

VIII. At this point, the participants form one large group. The facilitator asks the group recorders to give some of the positive and negative effects related in their group discussions. He asks the group members to relate their current attitudes and behaviors.

IX. The facilitator focuses the discussion on limiting the use of tests and reassessing the value or usefulness of standardized tests and test results.

Variations

I. An abbreviated session of systematic (deep) muscular relaxation may be used if the facilitator is skilled in its use. Several psychology books have manuals that can be followed.

II. The stimulus statements may focus only on the participants' later school experiences.

III. The stimulus statements may be assigned as homework for persons wishing to review and write about their previous positive and negative testing experiences. They can focus on some of the drawbacks in using standardized tests and test results.

IV. More focus may be given to the use and misuse of test results in steps VI, VII, and VIII.

V. The facilitator may shorten the session by using only selected portions of the stimulus statements.

Reference

Jones, J. E. Gunnysack: An introduction to here-and-now. In J. E. Jones & J. W. Pfeiffer (Eds.), *The 1973 annual handbook for group facilitators.* La Jolla, Calif.: University Associates, 1973.

47

Assessment by Vicarious Incentives: Objects and Persons

B. W. Van Riper

Goals

I. To provide an opportunity for the participants to examine similarities and/or differences in personal perceptions toward objects and persons.

II. To demonstrate to the participants the need for approaching assessment tentatively.

Group Size

No more than six to eight participants.

Time Required

Approximately thirty minutes.

Physical Setting

A room large enough to accommodate the participants.

Materials

I. A picture of an inanimate object (e.g., a bowl of fruit, a running brook, a forest glen) that is large enough for the group to view.

II. A picture of a well-known person (e.g., John F. Kennedy, Gerald R. Ford) that is large enough for the group to see.

Step-by-Step Process

I. The facilitator displays the picture of an inanimate object for viewing by the group.

II. The facilitator encourages each group member to describe to the group how he perceives the picture, i.e., what meaning the picture holds for him. He also asks each person to give the picture a title.

III. After each participant describes and names the first picture, the facilitator displays the picture of a well-known person.

IV. The facilitator asks each participant to relate briefly how he *feels* about the person in the second picture. Also, he asks the participants to use a descriptive adjective to describe what they think is the most important characteristic of the person in the picture.

V. The facilitator continues the discussion, focusing on the various perceptions and impressions, the disparity in viewpoints, and the reasons for common and divergent views.

VI. At this point, the facilitator emphasizes the tentativeness with which assessment should be approached. He reflects on the diverse nature of the participants' experiences and their reactions to the same stimuli.

Variations

I. The same process may be used with a large group of up to thirty participants; however, only some of the participants will respond to the pictures. They can be asked to write their responses for sharing in dyads, triads, or small groups.

II. The participants can be asked to compare first impressions to later impressions of objects and people. The influence of time and familiarity on perceptions of objects and people can be compared.

III. In step II, each participant may first give a name to the picture and the other participants can guess what significance the picture has for the person.

IV. Comparisons may be made of the kinds of words used by the participants to describe perceptions of the two types of pictures, e.g., feeling words vs. nonfeeling words.

Reference

Van Riper, B. W. From a clinical to a counseling process: Reversing the appraisal process. *Measurement and Evaluation in Guidance,* 1974, *7*(1), 24-30.

48

Assessment by Vicarious Incentives: Persons and Ideas

B. W. Van Riper

Goals

I. To demonstrate that personal attitudes and values often determine the way in which we judge people.

II. To help the participants review personal situations in which assessments are formed prematurely.

Group Size

No more than thirty people.

Time Required

Approximately thirty to forty-five minutes.

Physical Setting

A room large enough to accommodate the participants.

Materials

I. Paper and pencils.

II. Six quotations from well-known persons. The quotations selected should be thought-provoking, unconventional, controversial, or even antagonizing.

Step-by-Step Process

I. The facilitator distributes the paper and pencils and reads the first quotation. He asks the participants to respond in writing to the idea presented in the quotation. (Quotations may need to be repeated several times.)

II. Next, the facilitator asks the participants to describe in writing, preferably with a descriptive adjective, their perceptions of the person who wrote the quotation.

III. The facilitator repeats these two steps with the remaining five quotations.

IV. The facilitator collects the written responses and sorts them on the basis of several categories, such as negative and positive, emotional and unemotional, intellectual and quasi-intellectual, validating and nonvalidating, or new information and old information.

V. After providing feedback on the responses, the facilitator initiates a discussion on the effects of personal experiences, attitudes, and values in formulating opinions and judgments.

VI. The facilitator discloses the author of each quotation used in the activity. He continues the discussion by helping the participants examine personal situations in which judgments and assessments are arrived at too hastily.

Variations

I. The participants can be asked to view a TV stimulus presentation and to rate the presentation and the presenter on scales of one to five. They may be asked to correlate these ratings and to discuss the relationship between what a person says and how a person appears.

II. The facilitator might chose quotations with a specific topical area in mind.

III. When working with educators, anecdotes from cumulative educational records may be used in lieu of the quotations.

IV. Instead of responding to the quotations, the participants may be asked to match the quotations with the authors and to provide reasons for their choices.

49

ASSET:
A Student Self-Evaluation Tool

Kent D. Beeler

Goals

I. To provide an opportunity for students to evaluate their personal acceptance of responsibility for learning.

II. To provide feedback on how the members of the entire class evaluated their personal contributions to the advancement of their own learning experiences.

III. To permit individual students to see how they compared with the class in general by accepting responsibility for the learning in the course.

Group Size

Any number of students.

Time Required

Approximately fifty minutes.

Physical Setting

Any room in which the class meets.

Materials

I. A copy of the ASSET Questionnaire for each student.

II. Pencils.

III. Chalkboard and chalk or newsprint and a felt-tipped marker.

Step-by-Step Process

I. The instructor introduces the task with a brief discussion on the need for the students to become involved in self-evaluation for the enhancement of their own learning.

II. He distributes pencils and the ASSET Questionnaires and allows approximately fifteen minutes for the students to complete the instrument.

III. The instructor selects four of the items on the questionnaire to be utilized during the feedback and discussion session. (Questions 6, 8, 21, and 22 are suggested for consideration.)

IV. The instructor draws a sample profile chart on chalkboard or on newsprint that shows the frequency of responses to the various answers of each selected question. He records the students' responses by a show-of-hands procedure.

V. The instructor leads a discussion focusing on the four questions. The students will be able to review the responses of classmates to these four questions and will be able to compare their own responses immediately.

VI. Each student makes some sort of identifying mark on his questionnaire to remain anonymous. The instructor collects the questionnaires for scoring and preparation of a class profile.

VII. The instructor posts the class profile at the next class session.

VIII. He initiates a discussion on the students' overall responsibility for learning and the need for responsibility to be shared by the students and the instructor. At this point, the discussion may focus on ways in which the students and the instructor can share the responsibility for the teaching-learning process. Goals may be discussed for attitudinal and behavioral change in the teaching-learning process.

Variations

I. A shortened version of the ASSET Questionnaire can be given at timely points throughout the course to provide additional feedback to the students and the instructor.

II. Different items can appear in the ASSET Questionnaire depending on the nature of the course, the learning process, the format used, and the student population.

III. The students may be allowed to read the questionnaire at the beginning of the course so that they know in advance which areas of learning the instructor views as the domain of shared responsibility.

IV. The tool may be used in pre- and post-course evaluation processes to note student-instructor changes in attitudes and behaviors.

V. The evaluation tool may serve as a discussion stimulus for individual student-instructor conferences.

VI. The instructor may complete the evaluation tool with the total class in mind. Each individual's profile can be compared with the class profile. Inconsistencies can be noted and differences in perceptions discussed for possible readjustment of goals, impressions, and behaviors.

References

Beeler, K. D. Student educational self-evaluation: The other side of the coin. *New Directions in Teaching*, 1975, 4(4), 42-47.

Beeler, K. D. A student self-evaluation tool. *The Humanist Educator*, in press.

ASSET QUESTIONNAIRE
Kent D. Beeler

The purpose of this self-evaluation tool is to assess your commitment toward your own education and this course in particular. The results will be reported in a class profile at the next class meeting.

Please try to answer the questions sincerely. This is not a test; there are no "right" or "wrong" answers.

Background Information

1. Class Standing: ☐ a. Junior ☐ b. Senior
   ☐ c. Post-Graduate or Special Student
2. Sex: ☐ a. Male ☐ b. Female
3. Overall Grade-Point Average: ☐ a. Below 2.00 ☐ b. 2.00-2.49
   ☐ c. 2.50-2.99 ☐ d. 3.00-3.49 ☐ c. 3.50-4.00
4. College or School Enrolled in: ☐ a. Arts and Science
   ☐ b. Business ☐ c. Education ☐ d. Other

5. Did you look forward to taking this course?
   ☐ a. I had considerable interest.
   ☐ b. I had more interest than for most of my courses.
   ☐ c. I felt about the same as my other courses.
   ☐ d. I had less interest than for most of my other courses.
6. How would you rate your overall attitude toward this course?
   ☐ a. Highly positive.
   ☐ b. Vascillated, but still basically a wholesome one.
   ☐ c. Largely apathetic.
   ☐ d. Negative.
7. How would you describe the attitudes of other class members toward this course?
   ☐ a. One of the best they have taken.
   ☐ b. Above average.
   ☐ c. Average.
   ☐ d. One of the poorest they have taken.

8. How would you rate your attitude toward the subject field in general?
   ☐ a. Enthusiastic, enjoy taking such courses.
   ☐ b. Rather interested.
   ☐ c. Only routinely interested.
   ☐ d. Uninterested.

9. How would you rate your ability to relate with fellow students in committee or other-group work?
   ☐ a. No conflicts.
   ☐ b. Occasional conflicts.
   ☐ c. Conflicts seem to crop up somewhat regularly.
   ☐ d. Conflicts develop sooner or later.

10. How would you rate your tendency to listen to what others say in class?
    ☐ a. I give them my full attention.
    ☐ b. I listen most of the time.
    ☐ c. I am inconsistent in this.
    ☐ d. Only rarely do I pay that much attention to what is being said.

11. How would you rate your enthusiasm for becoming involved in class sessions and activities?
    ☐ a. I am usually one of the first to participate.
    ☐ b. My enthusiasm developed after initial sessions.
    ☐ c. Somewhat neutral.
    ☐ d. I avoid such involvement whenever possible.

12. Did you initiate any opportunities to get to know your instructor personally?
    ☐ a. I visited his office to ask questions or to discuss the subject.
    ☐ b. I talked with him before or after class.
    ☐ c. I talked with him on campus on a social basis.
    ☐ d. I had no contact with him beyond class meetings.

13. Did you think the instructor was trying to help the classmates advance their understanding of the subject field?
    ☐ a. He expressed considerable interest in doing so.
    ☐ b. He appeared to be trying to do an adequate job.
    ☐ c. He did not seem to care one way or the other.
    ☐ d. I did not notice any effort on his part.

14. When you were absent from a class, did you attempt to contact your instructor or another student for information about what you missed and/or what was planned for the next session?
    - ☐ a. I always made it a practice to find out.
    - ☐ b. Only if I suspected something important was missed or was planned.
    - ☐ c. I never bothered to find out.
    - ☐ d. I did not miss any class sessions.

15. In comparison with your classmates this term, how much have you studied for this course?
    - ☐ a. Much more than others.
    - ☐ b. Slightly more than others.
    - ☐ c. About the same amount.
    - ☐ d. Much less than others.

16. How much study time (clock hours) did you spend on this course for every hour of in-class session?
    - ☐ a. More than two hours.
    - ☐ b. About two hours.
    - ☐ c. More than one hour, but less than two.
    - ☐ d. Less than one-half hour.

17. In analyzing your contributions to the class, did you . . .
    - ☐ a. attempt to contribute regularly?
    - ☐ b. supply new information and relevant ideas?
    - ☐ c. seldom become involved?
    - ☐ d. never become involved?

18. Rate your punctuality for class sessions and appointments with the instructor or student study/work groups.
    - ☐ a. Always on time.
    - ☐ b. Late several times, but for legitimate reasons.
    - ☐ c. Late several times, but by choice.
    - ☐ d. Almost invariably late.

19. Rate the care with which you completed course papers and projects.
    - ☐ a. Neat final product.
    - ☐ b. Average attention to presentability.
    - ☐ c. Careless on occasion.
    - ☐ d. Consistently careless and sloppy.

20. How well satisfied are you with your own efforts in this course?
    - ☐ a. Very satisfied.
    - ☐ b. Moderately satisfied.
    - ☐ c. Average satisfaction.
    - ☐ d. Below-average satisfaction.

21. How much did the subject matter in this course stimulate your interest?
    - ☐ a. Very much.
    - ☐ b. Moderately.
    - ☐ c. Very slightly.
    - ☐ d. Not at all.
    - ☐ e. I am less interested now than previously.

22. Rate your acceptance of personal responsibility for the overall learning in this course.
    - ☐ a. Always fully accepted.
    - ☐ b. Usually fully accepted.
    - ☐ c. Partially accepted.
    - ☐ d. Sometimes refused.
    - ☐ e. Often refused.

23. To the best of my knowledge, my grade in this course will be a (an) . . .
    - ☐ a. A.
    - ☐ b. B.
    - ☐ c. C.
    - ☐ d. D.
    - ☐ e. Incomplete.

24. Considering all factors, my academic effort can be described as . . .
    - ☐ a. consistently the best work of which I am capable.
    - ☐ b. above-average most of the time.
    - ☐ c. rarely the quality of work of which I am capable.
    - ☐ d. little exertion on my part.

50

Removal of Barriers: A Closure Experience

Vincent Peterson

Goals

I. To provide an opportunity for a learning group to review what it recently has learned.

II. To deal with perceived barriers and to provide a basis for implementation of ideas and techniques into a participant's work setting and/or his own personal behavior pattern.

III. To enable the participants to leave a learning group with a positive plan of action.

Group Size

Any size learning group. The activity is prepared for high school-age participants and/or adults, but it can be adapted for younger groups.

Time Required

A minimum of one hour.

Physical Setting

A room large enough for the small groups to interact without disturbing each other. The participants should be able to sit in a small circle.

Materials

I. Pencils and two sheets of blank 8½" x 11" paper for each participant.

II. Chalkboard and chalk or newsprint and a felt-tipped marker.

Step-by-Step Process

I. The facilitator briefly mentions that this activity will help integrate the participants' learnings in the group and will leave them with a definite plan of action. He then distributes two pieces of paper and a pencil to each participant.

II. The facilitator instructs the participants to label one piece of paper "Ideas I want to use as a result of this learning group." He asks the participants to list on the paper all the ideas that they would like to pursue. Each item should be numbered, and both sides of the paper can be used. The ideas may relate to their work setting or personal growth. (Eight to ten minutes.)

III. After about eight to ten minutes, or when most of the participants appear to be finished, the facilitator instructs them to label the second sheet of paper "Barriers to action." He instructs the participants to list all the barriers that will hinder putting the ideas listed on the first sheet effectively into action. (Six to ten minutes.)

IV. The facilitator instructs the participants to place an asterisk (*) by each of the barriers that they believe to be insurmountable.

V. The facilitator asks the participants to draw a line through "barriers" that could easily be dealt with. (This step usually eliminates most of the barriers that are not starred.)

VI. The facilitator divides the total group into groups of four to six participants each. In these subgroups, each participant affirms publicly the ideas he plans to put into action. (Allow approximately five to ten minutes.)

VII. After each participant has announced the definite actions he plans to take, the barriers holding back other actions are listed on chalkboard or newsprint. The small group then brainstorms ideas to help circumvent the other barriers listed by each participant, starting with those that were not starred. (Fifteen to twenty minutes.)

VIII. If plausible ways of dealing with a perceived barrier are found and the participant accepts the idea that it is possible for him to put the idea into action, he should then affirm this intention to the group.

IX. The facilitator then asks the total group to reconvene. If time permits, each member of the various subgroups shares his plan of action with the total group. The learning activity then ends on a positive, constructive note.

Variations

I. Using legal-size paper lengthwise, "ideas" and "barriers" could be listed on the same page.

II. If the group is small, steps VI through IX may be conducted with the total group.

III. If time is available during step IX, it is often useful to list on chalkboard or newsprint the "insurmountable" barriers that still remain. The total group can brainstorm ways in which these barriers could be handled.

Suggested Background Readings

Aspy, D. N. *Toward a technology for humanizing education.* Champaign, Ill.: Research Press, 1972.

Beatty, W. H. (Ed.). *Improving educational assessment and inventory of measures of affective behavior.* Washington, D.C.: Association for Supervision and Curriculum Development, 1969.

Benjamin, A. *The helping interview* (2nd ed.). Boston: Houghton Mifflin, 1974.

Borton, T. *Reach, touch, and teach.* New York: McGraw-Hill, 1970.

Brown, G. I. *Human teaching for human learning: An introduction to confluent education.* New York: Viking Press, 1971.

Combs, A., & Snygg, D. *Individual behavior: A perceptual approach* (Rev. ed.). New York: Harper & Row, 1959.

Combs, A. W. (Ed.). *Perceiving, behaving, and becoming.* Washington, D.C.: Association for Supervision and Curriculum Development, 1962.

Combs, A. W., Avila, D. L., & Purkey, W. W. *Helping relationships: Basic concepts for the helping professions.* Boston: Allyn & Bacon, 1971.

Glasser, W. *Schools without failure.* New York: Harper & Row, 1969.

Gordon, T. *Parent effectiveness training.* New York: Peter H. Wyden, 1970.

Gorman, A. *Teachers and learners: The interactive process* (2nd ed.). Boston: Allyn & Bacon, 1974.

Greenberg, H. M. *Teaching with feeling.* New York: Pegasus Press, 1969.

Hamachek, D. (Ed.). *Human dynamics in psychology and education* (2nd ed.). Boston: Allyn & Bacon, 1972.

Johnson, D. *Reaching out: Interpersonal effectiveness and self-actualization.* Englewood Cliffs, N.J.: Prentice-Hall, 1972.

Jones, J. E., & Pfeiffer, J. W. (Eds.). *The 1973 annual handbook for group facilitators.* La Jolla, Calif.: University Associates, 1973.

Jones, J. E., & Pfeiffer, J. W. (Eds.). *The 1975 annual handbook for group facilitators.* La Jolla, Calif.: University Associates, 1975.

Jones, R. *Fantasy and feeling in education.* New York: University Press, 1964.

Jourard, S. *The transparent self* (Rev. ed.). New York: Van Nostrand Reinhold, 1971.

Krathwohl, D. R., Bloom, B. S., & Masia, B. B. *Taxonomy of educational objectives, Handbook II: The affective domain.* New York: David McKay, 1964.

Leonard, G. *Education and ecstacy.* New York: Delacorte, 1968.

Lyon, H. C., Jr. *Learning to feel: Feeling to learn.* Columbus, Ohio: Charles E. Merrill, 1971.

Maslow, A. H. *Toward a psychology of being.* New York: D. Van Nostrand, 1962.

Moustakes, C. *The authentic teacher.* Cambridge, Mass.: Howard A. Doyle, 1971.

Neill, A. S. *Summerhill: A radical approach to child rearing.* New York: Hart, 1960.

Patterson, C. H. *Humanistic education.* Englewood Cliffs, N.J.: Prentice-Hall, 1973.

Pfeiffer, J. W., & Jones, J. E. (Eds.). *A handbook of structured experiences for human relations training* (5 vols.). La Jolla, Calif.: University Associates, 1969-1975.

Pfeiffer, J. W., & Jones, J. E. (Eds.). *The 1972 annual handbook for group facilitators.* La Jolla, Calif.: University Associates, 1972.

Pfeiffer, J. W., & Jones, J. E. (Eds.). *The 1974 annual handbook for group facilitators.* La Jolla, Calif.: University Associates, 1974.

Pfeiffer, J. W., & Jones, J. E. (Eds.). *The 1976 annual handbook for group facilitators.* La Jolla, Calif.: University Associates, 1976.

Raths, L. E., Harmin, M., & Simon, S. B. *Values and teaching: Working with values in the classroom.* Columbus, Ohio: Charles E. Merrill, 1966.

Read, D. A., & Simon, S. B. (Eds.). *Humanistic education sourcebook.* Englewood Cliffs, N.J.: Prentice-Hall, 1975.

Rogers, C. R. *On becoming a person.* Boston: Houghton Mifflin, 1961.

Rogers, C. R. *Freedom to learn.* Columbus, Ohio: Charles E. Merrill, 1969.

Rogers, C. R. *Carl Rogers on encounter groups.* New York: Harper & Row, 1970.

Schmuck, R. A., & Schmuck, P. A. *A humanistic psychology of education: Making the school everybody's house.* Palo Alto, Calif.: National Press, 1974.

Simon, S. B., Howe, L. W., & Kirschenbaum, H. *Values clarification: A handbook of practical strategies for teachers and students.* New York: Hart, 1972.

Thayer, L. C., & Beeler, K. D. (Eds.). *Activities and exercises for affective education.* Ypsilanti, Mich.: Special Interest Group: Affective Aspects of Education (American Educational Research Association), Eastern Michigan University, 1975.

Toffler, A. *Future shock.* New York: Bantam, 1970.

Toffler, A. (Ed.). *Learning for tomorrow—The role of the future in education.* New York: Vantage Press, 1974.

Weinstein, G., & Fantini, M. D. *Toward humanistic education: A curriculum of affect.* New York: Praeger, 1970.

List of Contributors

Francis M. Aversano
Graduate Assistant
Educational Psychology &
    Research
Purdue University
South Campus Courts, Building G
West Lafayette, Indiana 47906

Margaret J. Barr
Assistant Dean of Students
University of Texas at Austin
Speech Building 103
Austin, Texas 78712

Kent D. Beeler
Assistant Professor of Education
Department of Guidance & Counseling
Eastern Michigan University
13 Boone Hall
Ypsilanti, Michigan 48197

Robert L. Bodine
Assistant Professor of Education
University of Wisconsin, Oshkosh
Department of Educational
    Foundations
Oshkosh, Wisconsin 54901

Lois Brooks
Visiting Lecturer
Department of Guidance & Counseling
Eastern Michigan University
13 Boone Hall
Ypsilanti, Michigan 48197

Carol A. Burden
Associate Professor of Education
College of Education
Drake University
Des Moines, Iowa 50311

Martin H. Crowe
Assistant Professor of Education
West Virginia State College
Institute, West Virginia 25112

Ajit K. Das
Assistant Professor
Department of Psychology
University of Minnesota, Duluth
320 Education Building
Duluth, Minnesota 55812

David L. Donahue
Associate Faculty, School of Liberal
    Arts (English)
Associate Instructor, Division of
    Education (Teacher Corps)
Indiana University-Purdue University
    at Indianapolis
902 N. Meridian Street
Indianapolis, Indiana 46204

Craig L. Dreilinger
Individual & Group Consultant
6081 Majors Lane, Apt. 10
Columbia, Maryland 21045

James A. Gold
Assistant Vice President for Student
    Affairs
University of Rhode Island
Taft Hall
Kingston, Rhode Island 02881

Geoffrey E. Grant
Management & Organizational
    Development Specialist
Executive & Management
    Development Branch
Division of Personnel Management
National Institute of Health
9000 Rockville Pike
Room B2C19, Building 31
Bethesda, Maryland 20014

Stuart N. Hart
Assistant Professor
School of Education
Indiana University-Purdue University
    at Indianapolis
902 N. Meridian Street
Indianapolis, Indiana 46204

Thomas H. Hawkes
Professor
Department of Psycho-Educational
    Processes
Temple University
Philadelphia, Pennsylvania 19122

Steven A. Heller
Division of Mental Health
1323 Winewood Boulevard
Tallahassee, Florida 32301

Paula K. Horvatich
Educational Consultant
School of Veterinary Medicine
Purdue University
West Lafayette, Indiana 47907

Russell Kraus
Provost Office
Whitmore Administration Building
University of Massachusetts
Amherst, Massachusetts 01002

Connie Farnham Kravas
Assistant Professor of Education
Department of Education
Washington State University
Pullman, Washington 99163

Konstantinos J. Kravas
Counseling Psychologist
Student Counseling Center
Washington State University
Pullman, Washington 99163

Cheng C. Liu
Assistant Professor
State University College at Buffalo
1300 Elmwood Avenue
Buffalo, New York 14222

Frederick H. McCarty
Associate Professor of Education
College of Education
Cleveland State University
Cleveland, Ohio 44115

Al Milliren
Assistant Professor of Elementary
    Education
Department of Curriculum &
    Instruction
Illinois State University
Normal, Illinois 61761

Richard G. Nelson
Assistant Professor
Department of Education
University of Rhode Island
Kingston, Rhode Island 02881

Bernard Nisenholz
Assistant Professor of Education
Division of Education
Indiana University at South Bend
1825 Northside Boulevard
South Bend, Indiana 46615

Vincent Peterson
Associate Professor of Education
Director of Counselor Education
Indiana University at South Bend
1825 Northside Boulevard
South Bend, Indiana 46615

Leslie Pettis
Systems Analysis
University of Michigan
Highway Safety Research Institute
Huron Parkway and Baxter Road
Ann Arbor, Michigan 48105

Charles M. Plummer
School of Education, Room 328
Indiana University
Bloomington, Indiana 47401

Judith A. Redwine
Director of Elementary Education
Indiana University at South Bend
1825 Northside Boulevard
South Bend, Indiana 46615

Gary F. Render
Assistant Professor of Educational
    Psychology
Department of Educational
    Foundations
College of Education
University of Wyoming
Laramie, Wyoming 82071

Edward W. Schultz
Associate Professor of Special
    Education
Program in Special Education
University of Maine
Farmington, Maine 04938

Louis Thayer
Associate Professor of Education
Department of Guidance & Counseling
Eastern Michigan University
13 Boone Hall
Ypsilanti, Michigan 48197

B. W. Van Riper
Associate Professor of Education
Department of Guidance & Counseling
Eastern Michigan University
13 Boone Hall
Ypsilanti, Michigan 48197

Bruce J. Yasgur
Social Studies Department
Central High School
Ogontz & Olney Avenues
Philadelphia, Pennsylvania 19141